THE BEST
OF
ST. THOMAS

"I want to be there, wanna go back down
and lie beside the sea there
with a tin cup for a chalice
fill it up with red wine
and I'm chewin' on a honeysuckle vine."

-- *Jimmy Buffett*

THE BEST OF ST. THOMAS

Pamela Acheson

TWO THOUSAND THREE ASSOCIATES
TTTA

Published by
TWO THOUSAND THREE ASSOCIATES
2003 Hill Street, New Smyrna Beach, Florida 32169

Printed in the United States of America

Cover Photograph: Pamela Acheson

Library of Congress Number 96-60152

ISBN 0-9639905-7-8

First Printing May 1996

For DCG and JK
We blinked, and already we're here.

ACKNOWLEDGEMENTS

Thanks to SA for design expertise and RHA for computer expertise. Special thanks to Pete Barnett. And more than thanks to MOTL, who made everything possible.

A DISCLAIMER

The author has made every effort to ensure accuracy in this book but bear in mind that despite what you hear about "island time" everything to do with vacationing in the Caribbean -- schedules, restaurants, hotels, events, modes of transportation, etc. -- can open, relocate, or close with remarkable speed. There are also still uncertainties about when and if some properties damaged by Hurricane Marilyn will ever reopen. The author visited damaged properties and talked with owners, and if it appeared that the property was being repaired this is mentioned in the text. Obviously, neither the author nor the publisher can be responsible for your vacation experience but we hope the experiences are wonderful.

INTRODUCTION

I love St. Thomas. It is unique – probably the only island in the world that is, at the same time, equal parts U.S. and Caribbean. It's foreign, yet oh-so-familiar. Traffic jams, fast food, and big hotels are combined with absolutely stunning tropical scenery, friendly and helpful local people, and an overall "island atmosphere" that is truly Caribbean.

St. Thomas is a wonderful island. In a single day you can swim in spectacular blue water, see stunning mountain-top views, engage in every water sport imaginable, visit a nearby island, dine elegantly under the moonlight, and end the evening in an intimate wine bar.

In September of 1995 Hurricane Marilyn smashed into St. Thomas. At the time I was back in the states in the final stages of writing this book. With news reports of mass destruction and no working phones, I worried for weeks about St. Thomas, her people, my many friends there . . . and, I must admit, the future of this book.

When I was finally able to fly back in early November, St. Thomas was a mess. In general the private homes were harder hit than the tourist areas, but happily the reports of mass destruction were most certainly greatly exaggerated. As this post-Marilyn book goes to press, St. Thomas's tourist industry is already back. The shops and resorts and restaurants, the natural beauty, the beaches and that blue, blue water – well, they're all here to enjoy.

The rapid "rebuilding" of St. Thomas was unbelievable. The people of St. Thomas rallied together to accomplish the impossible. Today as I wander about St. Thomas and exchange smiles and talk to people, I am amazed by this accomplishment, but I am even more amazed by the people. Many of them – from restaurant owners to bartenders to shopkeepers and cab drivers – lost virtually everything they owned when Marilyn visited their tiny island last fall. Yet her people endure and St. Thomas endures. I love this island.

– P. A., Charlotte Amalie, Spring 1996

TABLE OF CONTENTS

1. ABOUT ST. THOMAS 11

2. THE AREAS OF ST. THOMAS 15

3. GREAT RESORTS & INNS 21

4. GREAT RESTAURANTS 39

5. GREAT WINE BARS, QUIET & LIVELY BARS 57

6. GREAT SHOPPING 67

7. CHARLOTTE AMALIE LUNCH BREAKS 87

8. GREAT WATERSPORTS & BEACHES 95

9. GREAT ISLAND ATTRACTIONS 103

10. LITTLE ST. JAMES ISLAND 109

11. THE BRITISH VIRGIN ISLANDS FOR A DAY 115

SPECIAL FEATURES

Great St. Thomas Sights 19
Stuff You Probably Think You Don't Want to Do, But Might
    Be Glad You Did 20
Renting a Villa or Condo 35
Things People Usually Wish They Had Known Sooner 36
Things to Notice on St. Thomas 37
Did You Know? 38
The Chili Cookoff 52
Taxis and Taxi Drivers 53
The Old Airport 55
Some Great Bakeries, Delis, and Take-Out Food 56
The Most Original Bar 63
St. Croix for the Day 65
Charlotte Amalie Landmarks 68
Great St. Thomas Shopping Finds 72
Charlotte Amalie Shopping Locator 81
Art Galleries 84
Great Things to Look For 85
Local Knowledge 86
Always. . . 92
St. John for the Evening 93
Golf, Tennis, and Fitness Centers 101
A Full Day in Paradise 102
Tillet Gardens Art Center 108
Some Helpful Hints 112
Water and Hassel Islands 113
St. John for a Day 122
Kayaks and Little Power Boats 123
The Best of St. Thomas A to Z 124

Index 125
About the Author 128

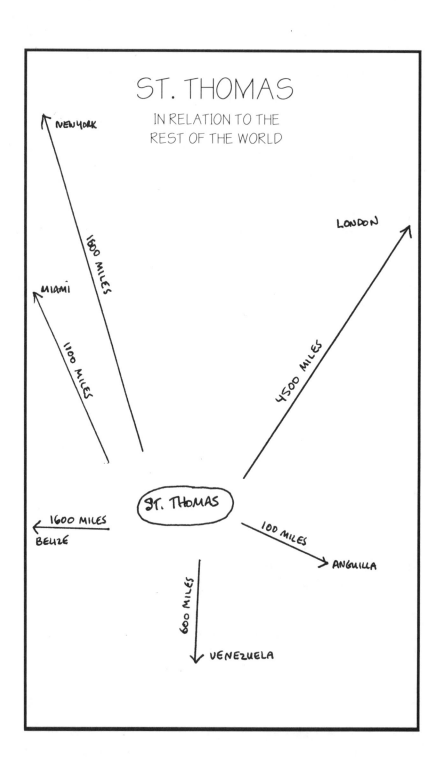

CHAPTER 1

ABOUT
ST. THOMAS

"I got to go where there ain't any snow,
there ain't any blow,
I got to go where it's warm."
-- *Jimmy Buffett*

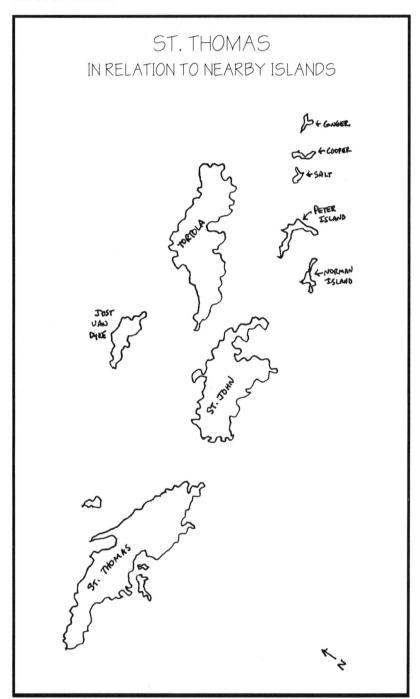

ST. THOMAS

What is St. Thomas?
It's one of the three main U.S. Virgin Islands. The other two are St. Croix, which lies 40 miles to the south, and St. John, which is less than three miles to the east. The USVI are a United States Territory.

How many other U.S. Virgin Islands are there?
Including rocks and cays, there are close to 60 U.S. Virgin "Islands."

How big is St. Thomas?
St. Thomas is the second largest of the U.S. Virgin Islands but it's only 13 miles long. Its width varies from one to four miles, but this narrowness is deceiving since you almost always have to go up over a steep hill to get to the other side.

What is the island like, geographically?
It's extremely hilly and lushly tropical. There is little flat land. Roads drop precipitously and hair-pin curves are the norm. Views are spectacular -- especially from the eastern end of the island which is a showcase for St. John and the British Virgin Islands. Beaches are postcard perfect strips of glistening white sand lined with graceful palm trees.

Isn't St. Thomas just for duty-free shoppers?
Charlotte Amalie in downtown St. Thomas is definitely one of the great duty free ports of the world, but it's also got lots of interesting little shops with one-of-a-kind items. Even people who hate to shop get smitten by certain stores downtown and elsewhere on the island. *See Great Shopping, page 67 for stores that are really special.*

What's special about St. Thomas?
Shopping is only a small part of what St. Thomas has to offer. Many people go there and never visit the shops. There are great beaches, wonderful drives, excellent restaurants and bars, sophisticated jazz spots, superb snorkeling and diving opportunities, parasailing, deep sea fishing, kayaking, and much more.

Can you visit other islands easily from St. Thomas?
One of the best things about St. Thomas is that it is so easy to take day trips to so many other islands. Choose a deserted cay or islet, or head to St. John or one of the British Virgin Islands. You can rent a little boat and drive yourself or you can join a sail or power boat excursion. You can also take a ferry to St. John or St. Croix or to several of the British Virgin Islands and wander about on your own.

What are the hotels like?
There are all kinds -- little inns, sprawling full-service beach resorts, luxury resorts.

Do I need a passport?
No, but you do need identification to come back to the U.S. mainland. A passport is always best, but an authenticated birth certificate or a voter's registration card is fine. You'll also need this if you want to visit the British Virgin Islands, which are an easy and delightful day trip.

Where is St. Thomas?
In the middle of a lot of water a long way from a continent. The closest continental spots are Florida, 1100 miles to the northwest; Belize at 1600 miles due west; Venezuela, which is 600 miles to the south; and northern Africa, 3300 miles to the east.

Is St. Thomas in the Caribbean Sea?
Actually, the Atlantic Ocean is on the north side of St. Thomas and the Caribbean Sea is on the south side.

Where is St. Thomas in relation to other Caribbean islands?
Puerto Rico is 50 miles to the west. Tortola, the largest British Virgin Island, is about 10 miles due east. Anguilla is about 100 miles due east.

What airlines fly to St. Thomas?
Delta (800-221-1212) and **American Airlines** (800-433-7300) are the major carriers.

CHAPTER 2

THE
AREAS
OF
ST. THOMAS

"The different areas of St. Thomas
almost seem like smaller 'islands'
within or perhaps on top of
the island of St. Thomas."

-- Richard Brooks

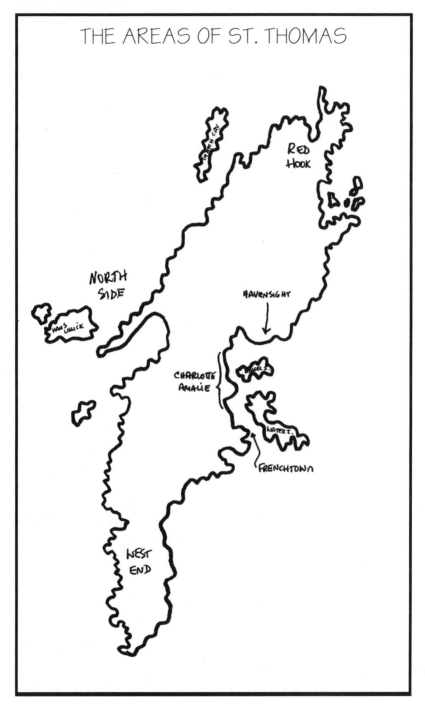

THE AREAS OF ST. THOMAS

THE AREAS OF
ST. THOMAS

Despite the fact that it is quite a small island, the areas of St. Thomas are remarkably diverse. Charlotte Amalie is a city of sorts, and the rest of the island is "out in the country."

CHARLOTTE AMALIE

There's a lot of fuss about the Charlotte Amalie cruise ship crowds, but what rarely gets mentioned is that this is actually a lovely city. It's nestled between steep green hills and a large harbor and many of the buildings here are quite beautiful. Look for brick walls and walls built out of skillfully placed stones, ornate iron grillwork gates and balconies, huge archways, and interesting shutters and doors.

Charlotte Amalie is little by any standards -- the true shopping area is less than half a mile long and only two blocks deep. Shops line the streets and alleys, but they are mixed in with a joyous collection of restaurants of all kinds.

FRENCHTOWN

Tiny but amazing Frenchtown is just around the corner from Charlotte Amalie, on the western edge of the St. Thomas harbor. It's on a little point of land with one inn and a remarkable number of restaurants of all kinds that are no more than a minute's walk from one another.

EAST END OF THE ISLAND AND RED HOOK

The east end of St. Thomas is hilly and tree-covered and the curvy shoreline is alternatively lined with sandy beaches and rocky outcroppings. Resorts are scattered along the shores but in most cases you can't really walk from one to the other unless you want to take a rugged hike.

Red Hook is the largest town on the east end of the island, but it's tiny compared to Charlotte Amalie and it has a character all its own. It's really laid back here. Although it's sometimes hard to find a parking spot, it never ever feels crowded. The town is right on a harbor and there are two little shopping complexes, one facing a marina and one across the street. There are very casual bars, several restaurants, and an excellent market. There is also a marina and a ferry dock, and ferries leave frequently for St. John and also for some of the British Virgin Islands.

NORTH SIDE

The highlight of St. Thomas' north shore is stunning Magen's Bay. Lush green hills sweep down to this magnificent turquoise blue bay and its three-quarter mile long stretch of glistening and palm tree-lined white sand. The houses scattered in the hills are residential or rentable villas and there are few restaurants on this side of the island.

WEST END

Many visitors don't ever realize that there is a west end of the island. There are no tourist areas here -- just farms and residential areas on steep, steep hills.

NEARBY ISLANDS AND CAYS

A number of little islands lie just off the shore of St. Thomas. Some, like Thatch and Grass Cay, are uninhabited. One of the great things about St. Thomas is that you can rent a little boat and visit one of these islands.

"I wish I told you how you
changed my life . . . the dreams
you made me dream again."

--*Aaron Neville, from* "I Owe You One."

GREAT
ST. THOMAS SIGHTS

THE SUN RISING ON THE BEACH

THE clouds you CAN ALMOST TOUCH

THE pelicans diving FOR THEIR dinner

THE AMAZING blues of THE WATER

THE lights of CHARLOTTE AMALIE

THE CRUISE ships HEADING OUT
IN TANDEM
AT THE END of THE day

THE MOON RISING OVER THE
ST. THOMAS hills

THE incredible colors of THE sky
WHEN THE SUN IS SETTING

THE seaplane TAKING off FROM THE HARBOR

Stuff you probably think you don't want to do, but might be glad you did. . . .

CATCH A SUNRISE
Sure, you're on vacation, but that's the point. You can get up early and enjoy one of nature's everyday miracles and not have to do anything. No work or school or appointments. Have a leisurely breakfast, take a walk, go back to sleep if you want.

WALK THE 99 STEPS
Okay it is exercise, but that's good. Walking up the steps gives you not only different views of St. Thomas but also a different feel. Plus at the top you can rest and have a cool drink or something good to eat at Blackbeard's Castle.

EAT WEST INDIAN
Try it at least once. It doesn't have to be dukunoo and bush tea. But you'll probably like kallaloo soup or johnny cakes or chicken rotis or conch fritters or funji. You only pass this way once.

TAKE A FERRY RIDE
Even if you don't like boats, even if you came down here only to lie on the beach, even if you just go to St. John and then return, try it. Let all your senses drink in the experience.

SWEAR OFF TELEVISION FOR YOUR TRIP
Blasphemy you say? Maybe not. Seinfeld or Baywatch or even Mystery will be on often through the end of this century. How often can you take a tropical moonlit walk, a night swim, or simply hold hands and gaze at the stars?

CHAPTER 3

GREAT RESORTS & INNS

"There is nothing which has yet been contrived by man by which so much happiness is produced as by a good tavern or inn."

--Samuel Johnson

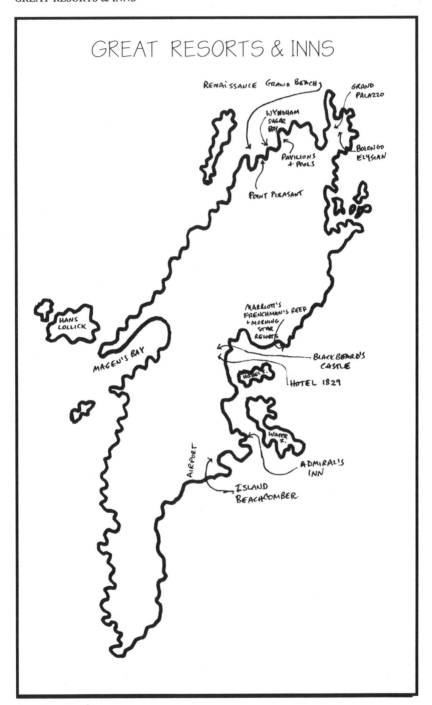

GREAT RESORTS & INNS

There are all kinds of great places to stay on St. Thomas: full-service resorts that you really never have to leave, intimate inns, motel-style beachfront hotels, condo-style units with full kitchens, and a wide range of rental villas. Hurricane Marilyn did some damage, but in most cases places are back to the way they were, only better (because so much was replaced).

Where you decide to stay on St. Thomas will depend a lot on what you want to do. Do you want to roll out of bed onto the beach, or spend the days visiting different beaches or exploring the island? Do you want to avoid shopping, or shop every day, or maybe just once? Do you want a big, full-service hotel with several restaurants right on the property or do you want a little inn? Or do you want the privacy of a villa?

Generally speaking, places to stay are either near Charlotte Amalie or about twenty-five minutes away, along the eastern end of the island. There are advantages to both locations. If you are near Charlotte Amalie, you are close to world-class shopping and many excellent restaurants. You are also near tourist attractions and not that far from famous Magen's Bay Beach.

If you choose the east end of St. Thomas, you are more "out in the country." You are close to a different set of excellent restaurants and close to the little town of Red Hook, which has limited but interesting shopping. Red Hook is where ferries leave frequently for St. John and the British Virgin Islands (less frequent service is also available from downtown Charlotte Amalie). You are also close to the departure point for many charter boat day trips and you are close to a number of very good beaches.

Rental villas are scattered all over the island and can be found on the beach and high in the hills. Many overlook stunning Magen's Bay. On the following pages are descriptions of some great places to stay.

Super-Luxury Resorts
There's one super-luxury resort on the island. When you want exceptional comfort and service, superb meals in elegant settings, and stunning views, this is definitely the place to come.

GRAND PALAZZO HOTEL

There is no question that this is the most luxurious resort on St. Thomas and one of the best in all of the Caribbean. Although there were reports that the hotel was destroyed by Hurricane Marilyn, in fact there was mainly some roof damage here and the hotel is scheduled to re-open September of 1996.

A gracious brick driveway lined with a profusion of brilliantly-colored tropical flowers leads to the formal entrance of this replica of a Venetian Palace. It's not until you reach the registration desk, though, that your gaze is drawn to a window and you get your first real look at this magnificent resort -- white stucco buildings lead out to a point on the right and below you, sweeping down to an exquisite pool, in what can only be called "perfect planting." Between the lawns and tropical flowering trees perfect walkways head hither and yon.

The 150 Junior Suites are plush and very civilized. Upholstered sofas provide a comfortable seating area. Wide french doors open onto a very private bougainvillaea-lined balcony when you want sunlight and views. Heavy draperies shut out light when you want to sleep. The comfortable king size bed is positioned so you can lie and look straight out at the view if you want. (A few rooms have two queens.) The pillows are excellent. There are spectradyne movies along with the television. The marble bathrooms are spacious and luxurious for the Caribbean, with heavy chrome bath fixtures, piles of plush white towels, and great water pressure.

The Palm Terrace and Cafe Vecchio restaurants were both excellent and are scheduled to reopen with the same staff. There is a half-mile of beach, a stunning pool, four tennis courts, an extensive health club, aerobic classes, and shopping shuttles to Charlotte Amalie. Several upscale boutiques sell sportswear and a 53-foot sailboat has daily sails.

By the way, after Hurricane Marilyn hit, the Grand Palazzo housed numerous employees who had lost their homes. *Great Bay. Tel.: 809-775-3333, 800-285-8666. Fax: 809-775-4444. General Manager: Marston J. Winkles. $$$.*

Luxury Full-Service Resorts
The resorts listed below have excellent service, very comfortable accommodations, and complete watersports programs, plus several restaurants and at least one shop on the property. They are all special.

ELYSIAN BEACH RESORT

What makes this spot extra-special is the combination of excellent service, spacious and contemporary units (many with full kitchens), appealing private grounds, and perhaps the most central location on the east end of St. Thomas. It's just a five-minute taxi ride to the little town of Red Hook and numerous restaurants are within a five- to ten-minute drive.

White four- and five-story buildings are clustered together on a hillside that sweeps down to a long crescent of beach. The 180 deluxe rooms and suites look out past beautifully manicured grounds to a picturesque harbor and St. James Island in the distance. Units are bright and spacious, with comfortable white-washed rattan furnishings and pale pastel fabrics. Suites have full kitchens and extra-spacious terraces, and some are duplexes with spiral staircases leading to a second-floor bedroom loft and a second private balcony. All rooms have air conditioning, televisions, and VCRs.

The free-form swimming pool has a waterfall (check out the secret underwater bench behind it) and the beach is a half moon of glistening white sand. Sailboats, kayaks, pedal boats, beach floats, snorkel gear, and even an introductory scuba lesson are complimentary. Tennis courts, an exercise room, and a large boutique round out the facilities. The beach bar has an all-day snack menu and offers amazing free snacks -- such as full-size hot dogs, as many as you want -- at Happy Hour.

The complimentary continental breakfast is a civilized sit-down affair and includes a delicious assortment of breads, muffins, rolls, croissants, and excellent doughnuts. There's a piano bar with weekend entertainment and the Palm Court is a pleasant restaurant open for lunch and dinner.

You never have to leave the property, but if you feel like venturing outside the Elysian, you'll find that you are in one of the best East End locations. Good restaurants are close by in virtually every direction and the town of Red Hook is practically around the corner. *Cowpet Bay. Tel.: 800-524-4746 or 809-775-1000. Fax: 809-776-0910. General Manager: Randall Doty. $$-$$$.*

MARRIOTT'S FRENCHMAN'S REEF & MORNING STAR

These two sister resorts, Frenchman's Reef and Morning Star, are at the opposite ends of the same property and share the same facilities. Together they form one giant, remarkably complete, full-service resort that you never, ever have to leave. There are seven restaurants, seven bars and lounges, duty-free shops, two pools, four tennis courts, a fitness center, an excellent unisex beauty salon, massage therapists, a great long beach, and a complete watersports program.

This dual resort was one of the first to re-open after Hurricane Marilyn. Damage here was primarily to the upper floors of Frenchman's Reef and its outside elevator. Even though restaurants and bars are open, reduced rates are in effect until the very last of the repairs are finished in the fall of 1996.

Frenchman's Reef and Morning Star are two completely different places to stay. Frenchman's Reef is a 481-room, eight-story hotel, along with several two-story wings, perched dramatically on a cliff. The duty-free shops, fitness center, swimming pools, and most of the bars and restaurants are also located here. Rooms are spacious and stateside-like and the rooms in the main building are virtually identical, except for the view. Most have excellent ocean views, some look out over the harbor (which is also pretty) and a few get only sky and parking lot. Choose Frenchman's Reef if you want to be close to everything and don't mind not being right on the beach.

Morning Star Resort is slightly more upscale and is the place to stay if you want to fall out of your bed onto the beach. The 96 rooms here are in a series of small three-story buildings that line the beach and are either oceanfront, ocean view, or garden view. Units are decorated in tropical decor and have large terraces or balconies. There are two restaurants and bars close by. Each resort has its own check-in desk, so be sure to tell your taxi driver which resort you are checking into. Ice makers and ironing boards in all rooms are a nice touch.

Restaurants offer Italian, Japanese, and American cuisine. The new pool complex has cascading waterfalls, fountains, jacuzzis, and a swim-up bar. There is a watersports program, and snorkeling, sailing, parasailing, and scuba diving trips can be arranged. *Frenchman's Bay. General Manager: Nick Pourzal. Phone: 809-776-8500, 800-524-2000. Fax: 809-774-6249. $$-$$$.*

POINT PLEASANT RESORT

This remarkable waterfront resort is nestled in dense greenery on the side of a steep hill. Great care has been taken not to disturb the environment. This is the place to stay if you love great views and like to walk through winding, woodsy trails. There isn't much of a beach (the shore is rocky here) but there's a beach next door and the pools here are superb.

You'd never know there are 134 rooms in this place. Units are in one- to four-story buildings discretely tucked here and there, surrounded by trees. Paths (some fairly steep) and wooden walkways lead from building to building, pool to pool, to reception and the restaurants, and off into the woods. Here and there along the walks there is a bench or a hammock to laze in.

Units have a gracious and welcoming feel, with wide expanses of glass that show off the view. Studio, one-, and two-bedroom units are available. All have full kitchens and many have great long terraces. The higher up you are, the more spectacular the views. Comfortable furnishings make these places that you can really settle into. All are air conditioned and have televisions.

The Agave Terrace restaurant is a popular dinner spot and the blackboard menu generally features five or six fresh "catches of the day." The casual Bayside restaurant sits outdoors on the rocky shore and is open from late morning until 8:30 pm. Hamburgers, salads, hot dogs, grilled chicken sandwiches and frozen drinks are the fare. You can order a full breakfast at the Agave Terrace or opt for the free coffee and danish served in the reception area. Three spectacular pools are at different levels with different views. Amazingly, you can almost always find an empty one -- people who stay here seem to be off doing things. The watersports' center offers complimentary windsurfers, snorkel equipment, little sailboats and, once a week, an introductory Scuba lesson. There's a small exercise room and a tennis court.

This is a resort that wants to make life easy for you. You can have a free car for up to four hours a day (there's a small insurance charge). There are shuttles to Charlotte Amalie and to Red Hook (five minutes away and a good place to get groceries) and evening shuttles to popular restaurants around the island. There's an activities desk, a gift shop with sodas and snacks, and a lending library. You can easily walk to the Renaissance Grand Beach, which is next door, for a beach and several more restaurants and bars. *Smith Bay Road. Tel.: 809-775-7200, 800-524-2300. Fax: 809-776-5694. Manager: Paul Royall. $$-$$$.*

RENAISSANCE GRAND BEACH

*Despite the fact that this 290-room, award-winning full service resort
sustained a tremendous amount of damage from Hurricane Marilyn it's
back to its former excellent self and also almost entirely brand new.
Rooms and restaurants are just where they used to be but almost
everything has been entirely redone.*

The Renaissance (which used to be the Stouffer Grand) is the northernmost
resort on the east end of St. Thomas. It's an upscale, AAA 4-Diamond resort
set among beautifully manicured lawns bordered by tropical greenery and
colorful flowers.

Rooms and suites are in a series of two- to four-story buildings that stretch up
a hill back from the beach. Rooms are spacious with wide balconies and most
have great views of the water and of nearby St. John and the British Virgin
Islands. Units have air conditioning, small refrigerators, televisions, and truly
excellent pillows.

The beach is a 1000-foot long arc of white sand with a complete watersports
program: jet skis, windsurfers, pedal boats, and snorkeling. The Chris Sawyer
Dive Center and a boutique are at the far end of the beach. The larger of the
two swimming pools is just off the beach along with a pool bar and a snack
bar. The more quiet, more private pool is set in tropical greenery.

There are three restaurants. Bay Winds and the adjoining Palm Cafe overlook
the beach and water. There is also a long bar here that looks out over the beach.
Smuggler's Restaurant is back among the palm trees and is the place to go for
Sunday brunch and their famous 12-foot long Bloody Mary bar.

In the reception building, you'll find a knowledgeable concierge who can assist
with everything from babysitters to menus of various restaurants. There's also
a tiny store selling liquor and snacks (the hotel's answer to mini-bars), and,
on the second level, a boutique, hair salon, and a shop with magazines,
newspapers, souvenirs, and sundries.

Service here is friendly and prompt, and it's a pleasure to stay here. By the
way, after the hurricane, this is another one of the hotels that gave free housing
to employees and 15 families of the Virgin Island Police Force that had been
left homeless by the storm. *Smith Bay. Tel.: 809-775-1510, 800-468-3571.
Fax: 809-775-2185. General Manager: John Murphy. $$-$$$.*

WYNDHAM SUGAR BAY RESORT

This is a popular full-service 300-unit resort with a beach, spacious and stateside-like hotel rooms, tennis courts, a complete watersports program, three connected pools with a waterfall, a few shops, several restaurants and bars, room service, and a program for children.

Wyndham Sugar Bay Resort rooms are in two tiers of rather imposing three-story buildings that crown a small hill. Rooms are large and comfortably furnished. Balconies are private and virtually all rooms have simply stunning views of nearby islands.

Rooms generally have either two queen beds or one king. The king bed is perfectly positioned so you can lie in bed and look out at a magnificent view. Rooms on the southwest side have stunning views of St. John. All rooms have ceiling fans and air conditioning, a coffee maker and small refrigerator, and a television with in-room movies.

It's a steep drop down to the pool and beach area, which you can get to by either walking or taking an elevator part way down. A swinging bridge crosses over the three interconnected free-form pools and there are great waterfalls you can swim under and hide behind.

The beach is narrow but adequate and you can snorkel, sunfish, jet ski, and windsurf, or just lie back and relax. There's a health club and spa, seven lighted tennis courts, and the island's only stadium tennis court (with seating for 220). A resident pro is on hand. Babysitters are available and there is a program for kids 12 and under.

There are two restaurants and a lounge with nightly entertainment. Sunday brunch and the Friday night Seafood Buffet are particularly popular. The town of Red Hook is five minutes away and there are a number of good restaurants close by. *Estate Smith Bay. Tel.: 809-777-7100, 800-927-7100. Fax: 809-777-720. General Manager: Rik Blyth. $$-$$$.*

> "Like some great wines,
> some great husbands
> do not travel well."
> *-- Anonymous*

An Inexpensive Resort
When you want to be on a beach, and don't want a pool or a fancy room or the numerous possibilities -- several different restaurants, entertainment, etc. -- offered by full-service resorts, this just might be the place.

ISLAND BEACHCOMBER

This is a casual resort almost across from the airport. It's informal, fun, and on a nice beach. This is a place where you can live in your bathing suit and bare feet and slip on a coverup for meals -- even dinner.

The airport is across the street but there aren't that many large planes that fly to St. Thomas so noise isn't a continual problem. The 50 air-conditioned rooms are in several two-story buildings. Some are beachfront. Others look out on tropical gardens. All are just a few steps from the beach. Rooms are comfortable and decorated in pastels. All have balconies or terraces, small refrigerators, and televisions.

The watersports center offers scuba diving, water skiing, and deep sea fishing. The beach is long and calm. Guests gather day and night at the casual beach bar and the beachfront restaurant serves breakfast, lunch, and dinner. It's a ten-minute ride to many excellent restaurants and downtown Charlotte Amalie. *Lindbergh Bay. General Manager: Dennis Cunningham. Tel.: 809-774-5250, 800-982-9898. Fax: 809-774-5615. $$.*

> **"If I had to do it again, I would try to accumulate**
> **more experiences.**
> **I would watch more sunrises,**
> **more sunsets,**
> **more moons push out of the sea.**
> **I would enjoy the sun and the rain and**
> **gaze more often at the stars."**
> -- from *My Life Again*

Intimate Inns
The best inns are close to Charlotte Amalie. None are on a beach,
but they do have pools, lots of charm, caring management, a cozy
atmosphere, and are near many restaurants and great shopping.

ADMIRAL'S INN

This is a wonderful place to stay if you want a casual spot and don't
mind not being on a beach. It's set on a point with great views of the
ocean, the harbor, and Charlotte Amalie. There's a nice pool. The
continental breakfast here is outstanding and you can easily walk to
great restaurants. The owners are exceptionally fine and helpful hosts.

Anne and Hal bought this informal inn in 1992 and have been improving it ever
since. It's built into the side of a little hill. There are 12 rooms in three pink
wooden buildings with bright red roofs. (This was a 16-room inn until
September of 1995 when Hurricane Marilyn blew away the entire second floor
of an eight unit building. Those two tall poles with flags flying from them used
to be the outside corners of the second floor.)

Rooms are light and airy and a comfortable size and modestly furnished in light
oak or rattan. The four ocean-view rooms are the highest and have private
balconies with a view of nearby Water Island and the Caribbean Sea. You'll
catch a glimpse of an occasional cruise ship crossing in the distance. These
rooms each have a king size bed. The eight harbor view rooms are in two
buildings that look out over St. Thomas harbor which, with the sparkling of
the downtown lights, is a particularly pretty nighttime view. These rooms have
one or two queen beds and terraces. There is also an efficiency apartment with
a small kitchen. All rooms have air conditioning, ceiling fans, and TVs. The
extra pillows are an excellent touch. Every morning coffee and juices and a
tempting assortment of exceptionally good homemade breads and muffins are
laid out near the pool. (Don't try to choose -- just give in and have one of each!)

The Admiral's Inn location is exceptionally convenient. Frenchtown restaurants are virtually "next door" and Charlotte Amalie is a long walk or a two
minute cab ride. The airport is an easy ten minutes away. The inn is also within
walking distance of the ferries to the British Virgin Islands. Car rentals are
nearby and will pick you up. Check for special dive, sailing, and honeymoon
packages. *Villa Olga, Frenchtown. Owners/Managers: Anne and Hal Borns.*
Tel.: 809-774-1376, 800-544-0493. Fax: 809-774-8010. $.

BLACKBEARD'S CASTLE

Why do people keep coming back to Blackbeard's Castle year after year? Because it's on a hilltop with a knock-out view of Charlotte Amalie and the harbor, because it's so peaceful that you can't believe you're anywhere near downtown, because the restaurant and bar are among the best on the island, and finally, because of owner Bob Harrington, who just seems to know exactly what people want. From the excellent menu to the civilized 12 noon check-out time, this inn is one of the best anywhere. Hurricane Marilyn certainly left her mark here, but soon after she hit, Bob had nine rooms re-opened and had built a temporary restaurant. By the summer of 1996, all should be back to the way it was but even better since the furnishings are all brand new.

This charming 24-unit inn sits high above Charlotte Amalie. The centerpiece is a National Historic Landmark, a five-story, beautifully crafted stone tower built in 1679 and believed to have been a lookout tower for the infamous pirate, Blackbeard. At the foot of the tower is a large swimming pool which stretches out to the edge of the hill and leads to a stunning vista of hilly green islands in St. Thomas harbor. There is a broad terrace around the pool and tropical flowers -- hibiscus, frangipani, and bougainvillaea -- everywhere.

Some rooms are larger than others but all are comfortable. Decor is eclectic and on the casual side. Some rooms have excellent views and others have none, so be sure to ask if you care. There are also three suites, each with a full kitchen, and two with huge windows, spectacular views, and a spiral staircase leading up to a bedroom loft. A continental breakfast is served poolside every morning.

The elegant restaurant (see page 46 for details) is one of the best on the island -- for casual lunches or romantic dinners. It's open to tropical breezes and looks out over the sparkling lights of Charlotte Amalie. The popular bar and piano lounge features light jazz six nights a week and a light bar menu.

If you want great food and a place in the sun, you never have to leave the "castle" but when you want to head downtown, you can just walk down the 99 steps to spend the day in Charlotte Amalie or catch a ferry to Morning Star beach. All rooms have television, ceiling fans, and air conditioning. Blackbeard's Castle is a sophisticated and relaxing spot -- it's very easy to be here. *Blackbeard's Hill. Tel.: 809-776-1234, 800-344-5771. Fax: 809-776-4321. Owner- Manager Team: Bob Harrington, Henrique Konzen. $-$$.*

HOTEL 1829

People often stay in this sophisticated historic inn because there's an excellent dinner restaurant and a wonderful bar on the first floor, because shopping and other restaurants are within easy walking distance, and because it has the warmth and friendliness you hope to find in a small establishment. Although there are only 15 rooms, the accommodations vary tremendously and range from luxurious to slightly spare.

The Hotel 1829 is located right on the eastern edge of downtown Charlotte Amalie, overlooking a park on Government Hill. A wide, steep set of stairs leads up to the original stone and stucco building, which was built by a French sea captain for his bride in 1829 and is now a National Historic Site. It's been a hotel since 1907. Graceful wrought-iron gates lead into the tiny reception area and into the comfortable bar and restaurant.

The 15 units vary tremendously in size, furnishings, and price and there really is something for everyone here. The fanciest units are quite beautiful. They are in the original building and are high-ceilinged suites with wooden beams, handsome stonework walls, upscale rattan furnishings, generous-size balconies, and views of the harbor.

The other suites and rooms are in a kind of compact sprawl that heads up a hill behind the original building and are reached by a narrow maze of outdoor stairways and walkways that crisscross charming tiny courtyards. These units are at various levels and are adequately but plainly furnished. Some look out at the small pool and others look out over the harbor, and some don't really look anywhere. A few rooms are extremely small.

All rooms have air conditioning and cable television and many have private balconies. There is a small and very private pool surrounded by a little courtyard.

A serve-yourself continental breakfast with juices, breads, and cold cereals is set up in the bar each morning and you can eat inside or outside on the balcony. Downtown and the waterfront are just a few steps away. *Government Hill. Manager: Torrie Newman. Phone: 809-776-1829, 800-524-2002. Fax: 809-776-4313. $-$$.*

PAVILIONS AND POOLS

You'll love this place if you have ever dreamed about being able to fall out of bed into your own very private pool -- one that you can swim in by the light of the sun or the moon. It's not a full-service resort and it doesn't have a beach (although one is a short walk away) but it does have great indoor and outdoor privacy.

Hurricane Marilyn popped the roofs off this place but it's due to be back just as it was, with a soft opening in the fall of 1996.

Pavilions and Pools is nestled on the east end of St. Thomas on a hill just above Sapphire Beach. Two long rather ordinary-looking buildings house rows of delightfully comfortable and very private apartments, each with its own personal swimming pool.

A fenced-in terrace around the pool affords true privacy. All you can see are trees and sky and you are visible to no one, except perhaps a passing bird. You are free to swim or float as naked as you wish, under the noonday sun or gazing up at the midnight stars. These pools are literally right next to both the living room and bedroom area and you can actually step right into the pool from either room, or sit at the edge of the room and dangle your legs in the water.

The units (and pools) come in two sizes. The International features a 20' x 14' pool and 1400 square feet of living space. The Caribbean has a 16' x 18' pool and 1200 square feet of living space. All units have an air-conditioned bedroom, living room, and full-kitchen, plus a shower nestled against a sunken garden. The larger units have a dining area and walk-in closets and a bigger shower-garden area. All units have a TV-VCR.

This is a wonderful place to completely relax. There's a video library and an informal little bar and very limited dinner service (one entree -- it might be bar-b-que ribs or steak or chicken) is prepared each evening except for Tuesday and Friday. Many restaurants (and an excellent grocery store) are five minutes away. If you feel like cooking, leave the dishes and don't feel guilty. Doing dirty dishes is included in the housekeeping service (do leave a nice tip if you leave a lot of kitchen messes). There's a daily shuttle into Charlotte Amalie. Long-time manager Tammy Waters does her best to make sure everyone has a great stay. *Smith Bay Road. Tel.: 809-775-6110, 800-524-2001. Fax: 809-775-6110. Manager: Tammy Waters. $-$$.*

RENTING A VILLA
OR CONDO

Some people think renting a villa is incredibly expensive, that villas are truly luxurious and only for the "rich and famous." Actually they are available in a wide range of sizes and prices, and many are competitive with resort rates.

Villas are wonderful if you want the convenience of a house -- privacy, ability to walk from one room to another, space, a full kitchen. Some families love them because everyone can "hang out" together around their own private pool (or even in the kitchen, just the way they do at home).

Off-season, "Lover's Special" rates make big fancy villas affordable for the couple that wants a romantic week away from real life or is celebrating an anniversary.

One of the advantages to renting a villa on St. Thomas is location. While most resorts are located on the east and south side of the island, villas are scattered all over. Many are on the north shore near beautiful Magen's Bay and others are high up in the hills, with unbeatable, airplane-like views of neighboring islands.

The absolutely best source on St. Thomas for villas and condos is McLaughlin Anderson. Call Nancy Anderson for a color brochure with photographs of the insides and outside of all the available villas. Also inquire about special packages. Tel.: 809-776-0635 or 800-537-6246 or 800-666-6246. Fax: 809-777-4737.

THINGS PEOPLE
USUALLY WISH
THEY HAD KNOWN
SOONER

Charlotte Amalie and a Beach
If you are staying near downtown Charlotte Amalie, an easy and enjoyable way to reach a beach is to catch "The Reefer," the little ferry that runs between the waterfront and Marriott's Frenchman's Reef Hotel (which is on Morningstar Beach). The ferry leaves the downtown waterfront (you can usually find it across from Bumpa's and Down Island Trader) on the half hour from 9am to 5:30pm. The trip takes about 15 minutes and costs $4.

Charlotte Amalie Hospitality Lounge
When you want an indoor pay phone, a rest room, a place to sit down, or tourist information, head to the Hospitality Lounge. You can also leave luggage here at $1 a bag. It's just off Waterfront Highway on Tolbod Gade (across from Vendors' Plaza). This place is run entirely by volunteers, so please leave a small donation if you can.

Stateside Papers
You can get current editions of *The New York Times,* the *New York Post,* the *Washington Post,* the *Miami Herald,* and the *Wall Street Journal* every morning at Island Newsstands in Charlotte Amalie.

Visiting St. John and the British Virgin Islands
It is really easy to head over to one of these islands for a day and it can be a great adventure, so build it into your schedule. Each island is different, so you can choose the one you think you'll like most. Or go with a group and see them all.

THINGS TO NOTICE
ON
ST. THOMAS

The tourists who didn't pack a carry-on. They are the ones
strolling the beach in their Brooks Brothers' suits.

The green flash as the sun settles into the Caribbean.

Shooting stars and satellites – if you gaze at the night sky
for fifteen minutes you'll see at least one. Guaranteed.

How close the stars look – as if you could just reach out
and touch them.

Phosphorus lighting up the night sea.

The delightful donkey at Drake's Seat.

Iguanas – they are a little ugly but they know
how to relax.

Beautiful hummingbirds hanging around
the hibiscus blossoms.

DID YOU KNOW?

St. Thomas is on the same geologic shelf as the British Virgin Islands and Puerto Rico. It is thought that several times in the last 60 million years you could probably have walked from one island to another on dry land.

St. Thomas is 18 degrees north of the equator.

If you headed straight east, you'd cross the British Virgin Islands, the island of Anguilla, and then, 3,000 miles later, the Cape Verde Islands off the coast of North Africa.

If you walked along St. Thomas' curvy coastline until you got back to where you started, you would have walked almost 60 miles.

The turpentine tree is distinctive-looking, with red-orange bark. It's sometimes called the "tourist tree" because its skin is constantly peeling.

The machineel tree can be a real pain. It bears small green apples which are poisonous. Its sap and bark can cause painful blistering that feels just like a bad burn. Don't even stand under the tree in a rain – water dripping from the leaves will burn your skin.

The reason there are so many stairs outside in Charlotte Amalie is that the Danes laid out plans for the city back in Denmark and thought the land was flat. When it came time to build, everywhere it was just too steep to put a street, they had to build a stairway instead.

CHAPTER 4

GREAT RESTAURANTS

"Part of the secret of success in life
is to eat what you like and
let the food fight it out inside."

--Mark Twain

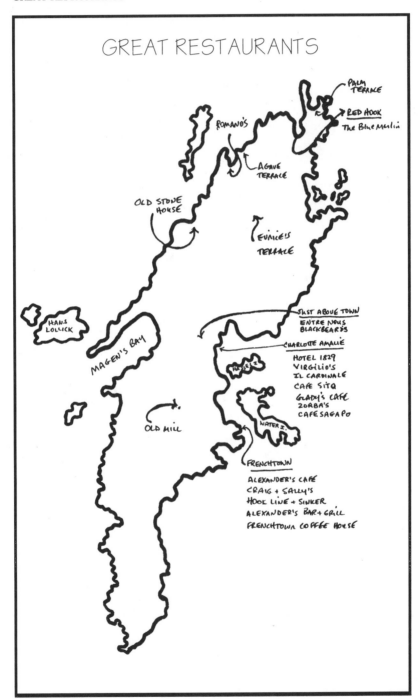

GREAT RESTAURANTS

PALM TERRACE

RED HOOK
The Blue Marlin

ROMANO'S

AGAVE TERRACE

OLD STONE HOUSE

EVALIE'S TERRACE

HANS LOLLICK

MAGEN'S BAY

JUST ABOVE TOWN
ENTRE NOUS
BLACKBEARDS

CHARLOTTE AMALIE

HASSEL I.

HOTEL 1829
VIRGILIO'S
IL CARDINALE
CAFE SITO
GLADY'S CAFE
ZORBA'S
CAFE SAGAPO

OLD MILL

WATER I.

FRENCHTOWN

ALEXANDER'S CAFE
CRAIG + SALLY'S
HOOK LINE + SINKER
ALEXANDER'S BAR + GRILL
FRENCHTOWN COFFEE HOUSE

GREAT RESTAURANTS

St. Thomas has many great restaurants. Some are elegant and some are casual. Some are air-conditioned and indoors and some are open to the Caribbean breezes and look out at great nighttime views.

St. Thomas is a sophisticated island and there are many highly-skilled chefs here who demand high-quality and unusual ingredients. On St. Thomas you can expect to find some of the best food anywhere. You will find all kinds of cuisine -- Italian, German, Continental, Greek, Spanish, and West Indian. Local fish you can expect to see on the menu include wahoo, mahi mahi, swordfish, and tuna.

Most restaurants on St. Thomas are either clustered in Charlotte Amalie and Frenchtown (which is just around the corner from Charlotte Amalie) or are out on the east end of the island in or near Red Hook. In the evening it's about a 20-25 minute ride between the two areas. Taxi fare is $7.50-$9 per person. The same taxi that takes you to your restaurant will pick you up also, if you want.

One of the most magical and enchanting features of the Caribbean is the ability to have elegant meals on terraces that are open to the outdoors. In harsher climates fine china and crystal, gracious service, and gourmet cuisine are almost always associated with a climate-controlled, indoor environment. But in the Caribbean one can combine a sophisticated and refined style of dining with soft breezes and romantic nighttime scenery -- sparkling stars, rising moons, twinkling distant lights.

Restaurant prices in St. Thomas are not that different from prices in cities on the mainland. The restaurants on the following pages do not include price guidelines. Generally, on St. Thomas, the fancier the restaurant is the more expensive it is. However, lobster is expensive everywhere. In general, the amount of your check will reflect what you ordered more than where you dined.

GREAT ELEGANT RESTAURANTS

VIRGILIO'S

Virgilio's is one of the very best restaurants in St. Thomas and perhaps anywhere. Exceptional northern Italian cuisine is served indoors in an elegant, intimate atmosphere.

Walk into this dark and cozy restaurant and the rest of the world melts away. Two-story exposed brick walls are hung with a marvelous mix of all sizes of framed paintings and prints. Although tables are quite close together, in most cases, once seated, you forget you have neighbors.

The exceptional menu offers everything from veal saltimboca to chicken cacciatora, grilled filet mignon, and capellini with a fresh tomato sauce but, before you order, be sure you've heard the daily specials. And if what you want is not on the menu, do ask. There is an extensive wine list with many excellent, inexpensive Italian wines, but if you feel like splurging you can always order the Biondi-Santi Brunello Reserva 1945 for $2,500. Don't leave without trying a Virgilio's Cappuccino, a special blend of coffee and Italian liqueurs and a pleasant ending to any meal.

Although Virgin Island power lunches are held here, Virgilio's is really meant for lingering. Come here anytime for great food and also when you feel like having a romantic dinner or a leisurely late lunch with a bottle of fine champagne. There's a tiny four-seat bar. Reservations are a must. Closed Sunday. *Downtown Charlotte Amalie on Storevater Gade, between Main and Back Street. Tel.: 776-4920.*

"THERE IS NO LOVE
SINCERER
THAN
THE LOVE OF FOOD."
-- G.B. SHAW

HOTEL 1829 RESTAURANT

Long considered one of St. Thomas' best restaurants, the Hotel 1829 offers a sophisticated menu in a refined and peaceful terrace setting.

Elegantly-set tables line the outdoor terrace of this historic landmark. The breezes are soft and the lights of Charlotte Amalie sparkle through the trees. The menu runs the gamut -- basil linguini with jumbo shrimp, grilled swordfish, Moroccan-style chicken, medallions of wild boar. Two tableside flambed dishes, the wilted spinach salad for two and the filet mignon with pepper sauce are house specialties here, as are the dessert souffles (the chocolate and Grand Marnier are outstanding).

Service is excellent and if you are in the mood for something special, there's Sevruga and Beluga caviar, a humidor of fresh cigars, and a variety of ports, aged rums, and calvadoes. The prix-fixe lunch, which is served from 11am to 2:30pm, includes an appetizer, entree, and dessert. Reservations necessary for dinner. *Downtown Charlotte Amalie. Government Hill. Tel.: 776-1829*

ENTRE NOUS

For excellent cuisine in an exceptionally romantic outdoor setting, nothing on St. Thomas beats elegant Entre Nous.

Liz and Jerry Buckalew's Entre Nous has been one of St. Thomas' best restaurants for close to 20 years. It's at Bluebeard's Castle on a hill overlooking Charlotte Amalie and the harbor.

Tables are well-spaced on a broad covered terrace open to the Caribbean breezes and at night the twinkling lights below are simply magical. (One of the great sights here is seeing the full moon rise over the hills of St. Thomas.) But the food and the service are every bit as good as the view.

Guests come back year after year to dine on the famous tableside Caesar salad, Chateaubriand, and Rack of Lamb. The potato chowder is excellent and, if you feel like something light, try the goat cheese with greens and grilled vegetables -- it's also a beautiful presentation. Sorbet here is good and Bananas Foster is a house specialty.

There's a cozy little bar at the entrance. Reservations necessary. Dinner only. Closed Tuesday. *Bluebeard's Castle on Bluebeard Hill. Tel.: 776-4050.*

IL CARDINALE

This restaurant is in a restored 200-year old building that was once a Moravian Church. A brick stairway leads up to this quiet second-floor indoor spot where you can dine on fine northern Italian cuisine.

Windows look out at tree tops and large European paintings adorn the walls in this small and quiet two-level restaurant with intimate tables and comfortable banquettes.

The menu features many veal and chicken dishes and a long list of pasta but order whatever you want here. Owner Rene Davidovici, who most likely will greet you at the door, considers the menu to be just a suggestion. Four main course specials are offered every day. The grilled portobello mushroom -- which is not on the menu -- is an excellent appetizer and the vegetarian Involtini di Melanzane (thin slices of eggplant wrapped around ricotta, parmesan, pine nuts, and raisins in a plum tomato sauce) is delicious. The creme caramel, tiramisu, and amaretto cheesecake get high marks for dessert.

There's a small outdoor bar. Reservations are necessary for dinner. Closed Sunday. *Downtown Charlotte Amalie on Back Street, in the Taste of Italy complex. Tel.: 775-1090.*

ALEXANDER'S CAFE

Excellently-prepared German and Austrian cuisine is served side by side with grilled fresh fish, excellent pasta, and extra-healthy low-calorie "spa" dishes at this stylish, sophisticated spot.

The walls are pink, the furnishings are lacquer black, the tablecloths are crisp and white, and the overall effect is striking. This is a very small restaurant with a superb chef, a classy atmosphere, and a remarkably varied menu.

You can come here for excellent smoked pork loin, authentic weiner schnitzel, or a plate of German sausages. You can have pasta with several excellent sauces including a ripe tomato sauce and a quite good pesto, or you can choose from the low-calorie spa menu, which includes a grilled chicken breast on a bed of grilled vegetables and a spinach salad with grilled shrimp. There are several kinds of caviar and a large wine list. In the back is a small bar. Reservations are a good idea in season. Closed Sunday. *Frenchtown Mall. Tel.: 774-4349.*

PALM TERRACE

This restaurant is at the Grand Palazzo Hotel which was damaged by Hurricane Marilyn and is scheduled to re-open in September 1996. The Palm Terrace was the most elegant restaurant on St. Thomas and is sure to be again. The restaurant itself was minimally damaged and the same staff will run it when it re-opens.

This restaurant looks out over the water to the sparkling lights of St. John. The service, cuisine, and ambiance were superb here. A classical pianist performed nightly. Dinner was an elegant and restful experience. The classical piano music was just wonderful to dine by. Call and see if they have opened yet. Dinner only. Reservations necessary. *Grand Palazzo Hotel, Great Bay. Tel.: 775-3333.*

ROMANO'S

This is THE PLACE in season and reservations are a must to dine at Tony Romano's swank northern Italian restaurant.

A huge number of interesting paintings and watercolors are hung along the walls of this slightly bright, very upscale East End restaurant. Fresh flowers are on the table and the service is professional.

The menu is classic (and not so classic, but equally delicious) northern Italian. Lingua di Bue Brasta (veal tongue) and Ossobucco are the most popular dishes here. The roasted garlic and red and yellow pepper soup (which isn't usually on the menu but might be a special when you are there) is superb. Among the pasta dishes, the Penne Pianello (penne with mushrooms, proscuitto, pine nuts and cream) and the linguini with broccoli are excellent.

Look for Tony. He's usually working hard in the kitchen, but he often wanders out toward the end of the evening to greet his guests.

This is one of the most popular restaurants on St. Thomas and you may have to wait a bit in season, even if you have a reservation. There's a little terrace where you can have a drink but it's far more interesting to sit at the bar and check out the huge number of interesting spirits and grappas that crowd the shelves. Closed Sunday. Dinner only. *6:30 to 10:30. Coral World Road, Smith Bay.* Tel.: 775-0045.

BLACKBEARD'S

This peaceful spot sits up on a hill overlooking Charlotte Amalie and is open to the soft Caribbean breezes. The view at night -- twinkling lights in the distance -- is magical. Hurricane Marilyn did a number here but everything should be up and running by the summer of 1996.

This is one of the most popular spots on the island. You can choose to dine outdoors under a canopy or almost outdoors in a room that is completely open to the breezes from waist-level to ceiling. Tables look out over Charlotte Amalie and the harbor. Dinner is romantic and intimate here, with soft lighting and a view of the sparkling nighttime lights of downtown.

Come here for a mixed grill, poached Caribbean lobster tail, grilled vegetables with whole wheat fettuccine, or tournedos of beef tenderloin with garlic and sun-dried tomatoes. The variety on the menus and the mixture of cuisines here is just delightful. For example, at lunch it's a treat to be able to choose either black bean soup or a roast beef on rye or cheese tortellini or a chicken stir-fry. This is a terrific spot to come for a Sunday brunch; the a la carte brunch menu has something for everyone -- from pumpkin pancakes to eggs benedict to a mixed green salad with poached salmon to a juicy hamburger. There is also a comfortable lounge (see page 60). *Government Hill. Tel.: 776-1234.*

OLD STONE HOUSE

The setting is magnificent -- three rooms in an old stone house with magnificent stone walls, wide plank floors, and, all along one wall, graceful arches open to the breezes and tropical greenery. Hurricane Marilyn took away the roof but this spot is sure to be back in business and better than ever. The owner and chef is a well-known and very successful St. Thomas restauranteur.

This beautiful house was originally a plantation Great House 200 years ago and it's the perfect setting for an elegant restaurant. Tables are well-spaced, service is professional, and the live piano music provides a relaxing background. The menu is contemporary and creative -- squash soup with a dollop of pears, grilled pork and grilled duck, fruit sorbets. This is the place to come for excellently prepared creative cuisine in a refined setting. The wine list is extensive. Reservations necessary. Closed Sunday. *North side of the island. Route 42 at Mahogany Run. Tel.: 775-1377.*

GREAT CASUAL RESTAURANTS

CRAIG AND SALLY'S

Two owners that really care, a great menu, and excellent food served in a casual but cosmopolitan atmosphere make this Frenchtown place worth coming back to again and again.

There are seascape murals on the walls, five or six different dining areas, and comfortable low lighting. Craig and Sally love to run a restaurant and it shows. Nobody cares if you just want to order the Caribbean quesadilla appetizer. In fact, the wait-staff will tell you it's a big dish and caution you from ordering anything else. (It is big, but also delicious -- try it with a salad.)

What's good here? Everything. Try the grilled swordfish with sun dried tomatoes, or the twice-baked lobster-stuffed potato. There's an excellent grilled breast of duck with tangerine sauce, a tender chicken breast stuffed with goat cheese, and various pasta dishes. Sooner or later you'll notice that crates of wine are stacked here and there all over the place. Craig enjoys wines and likes to offer ones that are truly unusual. Check and see what he's got when you're on the island. There's a large, comfortable bar also. Reservations are a good idea in season. Closed Monday. *Frenchtown Mall. Tel.: 777-9949.*

CAFE SITO

Even though this faces the Charlotte Amalie waterfront, this could definitely be a cafe in Spain. Come here and relax over several orders of delicious tapas or have a complete meal. The outdoor patio is very casual. Indoors is slightly more formal.

An iron gate leads into the casual patio of this charming little restaurant that faces the harbor in Charlotte Amalie. Sit outdoors under an umbrella or indoors in air-conditioned coolness. You can have a complete lunch or dinner or just relax with a bottle of wine and sample various tapas (sort of like appetizers -- small portions of delicious concoctions), one at a time. There are quite a few hot tapas -- some of the best are the grilled scallops with caramelized onions; a pastry tower stuffed with chicken, roasted peppers, and mushrooms; and roasted garlic and brie wrapped in phyllo dough. Other great menu items include a zesty gazpacho, a spicy chicken and chorizo sausage paella, and a roasted pork loin wrapped in bacon. *In Charlotte Amalie, just west of the Hard Rock Cafe on Waterfront Highway. Tel.: 774-9574.*

THE BLUE MARLIN

When you want truly fresh fish, one of the best places to head to is this pleasant spot which overlooks the marina on the east end of St. Thomas.

Big blue marlins decorate this blue restaurant that looks out over the water. Come here for really fresh fish in a casual, comfortable setting. Swordfish, wahoo, tuna, and mahi mahi come right from the docks. Try the tuna pan-seared with caper berries and balsamic vinaigrette, or the grilled marinated swordfish. Garlic mashed potatoes are excellent here. There's a nightly pasta special which you can have either as an appetizer or a main course. Desserts are popular here. Save room for the sweet fruit pizza, or the homemade blueberry or apple pie. Chocolate lovers will love the chocolate sponge cake rolled around whipped cream. Mark Hitchin, the owner, used to own the charming Mark's Parkside restaurant and it's nice to have him back in this new location. No lunch Saturday. Sunday brunch instead of lunch. *Red Hook at the marina (where Piccola Marina restaurant used to be). Tel.: 775-6350.*

ZORBA'S AND ZORBA'S CAFE SAGAPO

Two casual Charlotte Amalie restaurants -- but one kitchen and one excellent menu. Greek dishes -- including very light ones -- and crisp pizzas are served in an appealing indoor cafe or on a breezy terrace.

Cafe Sagapo is indoors and Zorba's is on a terrace out back but the menu is exactly the same. (As Jim Boukas, the Greek owner of both, explained, he tried two menus but people coming to either restaurant always wanted "just one thing"off the other menu. Now he makes both menus the same.)

Distinctive purple and turquoise shutters frame the open windows of inviting Cafe Sagapo. Inside it looks like a traditional Greek coffee house. Banquettes run along the walls, comfortable pillows are scattered about, and Greek rugs adorn the exposed brick and stone walls. There's a little bar and often a guitar player on weekend evenings. Zorba's is a peaceful oasis out back on a covered terrace, with views of a waterfall and dense foliage. The crisp pizzas, the best on St. Thomas, are cooked in a woodburning oven. Greek specialties here include a tasty mousaka, avogolemono soup, gyros, and spinach and feta pie. You can make a meal out of the hot and cold appetizers here and there are a number of vegetarian items. In the morning, stop by anytime after 7:30am for some Greek toast and cappuccino. Bread here is exceptional (you can buy it by the loaf -- the olive is the best). *Downtown Charlotte Amalie on Government Hill. Tel.: 776-0444.*

AGAVE TERRACE

Dining here is on a little terrace or in a breezy room with open walls. Fish is the specialty here at this hillside spot. It can be quite busy, especially on season.

Check out the blackboard as you walk onto the terrace entrance of this popular seafood restaurant. The specialty here is fresh fish and the blackboard reports the day's choice of catches -- four or five fresh fish daily -- prepared grilled, pan fried, blackened, baked, or batter fried. If you've spent the day catching your own on a deep-sea fishing trip, they'll be happy to cook your catch.

The menu also includes grilled steaks, a grilled chicken breast, a number of steak choices, and several chicken dish choices including linguini with chicken. The view from the terrace and the bar is spectacular. It looks out toward St. John and the British Virgin Islands. *East End on Smith Bay Road at Point Pleasant Resort. Tel.: 775-4142.*

THE OLD MILL RESTAURANT

A young crowd heads to this casual Italian restaurant which serves dinner 365 days a year. It's part of a popular late-night bar and restaurant complex five minutes west of Charlotte Amalie.

Latticework hung here and there between clumps of trees act as informal walls for this outdoor restaurant on Contant Hill. The atmosphere is casual and appealing, with dim lighting and tropical greenery around. The menu includes Caesar Salad (either by itself or with grilled chicken or shrimp), various pasta dishes (including spaghetti and meatballs, sausage, or meat sauce; lasagna; baked penne and marinara sauce; chicken tossed with penne) plus grilled fish and steaks, and pizzas. Dinner is from 5-11 but there's also a late night menu from 11pm until about 4am, with burgers, subs, hot dogs, and pizzas. *On Contant Hill, about five minutes west of Charlotte Amalie. Tel.: 776-3004.*

HOOK LINE AND SINKER

A truly great restaurant masquerading as a coffee shop might be the best way to describe this Frenchtown spot.

The building is attractive weathered wood outside, and inside it's an upscale coffee shop, with booths along the walls, simple tables, and a counter where you can eat. Windows are open to tropical breezes and you can see pelicans diving for food. This is the kind of place that you could come to seven days in a row and have something different and it would all be good. Hamburgers (available lunch and dinner) are great but so are the lunchtime sandwiches. There's a terrific Reuben and also a great Black Russian (pumpernickel plus corned beef, turkey, and coleslaw). For dinner, choose pasta dishes, or fresh fish such as grilled swordfish or pecan-coated red snapper, or London Broil with homemade mashed potatoes. Check the blackboard for great daily specials like meatloaf and mashed potatoes or their excellent Chicken Popeye Salad. Open for brunch only on Sunday 10-2:30. *Frenchtown. Tel.: 776-9708.*

ALEXANDER'S BAR AND GRILL

This is a "plain old bar" actually, but with terrific dinner specials.

This is a regular bar -- dark, smoky, sports on the TV, regulars sitting at the bar -- with tables along the wall. It's a great bar. But it's included here under great restaurants because the Blue-Plate dinner specials are really excellent. They change nightly and range from spaghetti and meatballs to meatloaf and mashed potatoes. When you want to sit at a bar and have a satisfying meal, this comes close to being perfect. There are tables also, as well as a menu. You can get chili, hamburgers, an excellent grilled chicken club sandwich, and some German and spa dishes similar to those at Alexander's (same owner -- see above). Closed Sunday. *Frenchtown Mall. 774-4349.*

FRENCHTOWN COFFEE HOUSE

Come here for the absolutely best coffee on St. Thomas.

The atmosphere here is welcoming, with Oriental rugs on the floor and photographs and artwork on the walls. Stop here for coffee, espresso, bagels, and breakfast muffins. You can also step into the deli next door for a sandwich and eat it while perusing the latest editions of the *Wall Street Journal* and *The New York Times. Frenchtown Mall. Tel.: 776-7211.*

GREAT WEST IND.IAN FOOD

GLADYS' CAFE

This is a very casual outdoor cafe for breakfast, lunch, and dinner that looks out over the harbor and has good food.

Gladys has owned several restaurants since she moved here from Antigua in 1969 and her latest location is right in downtown Charlotte Amalie on Waterfront Highway. This is definitely a place to try West Indian specialties.

Gladys is famous for her curried chicken and also known for her chicken soup with pigeon peas, pan-fried yellow tail with Creole sauce, and lemon-buttered conch. You can also get meatloaf with real mashed potatoes, a green salad with a grilled breast of chicken, and hamburgers. Tired shoppers like to relax with one of Gladys' special soursop coladas. *Downtown Charlotte Amalie on Waterfront Highway at Royal Dane Mall. Tel.: 774-6604.*

EUNICE'S TERRACE

For the best conch fritters on St. Thomas, head to this large, informal, and rather busy restaurant close to Smith Bay on the east end of St. Thomas. The specialty here is West Indian cuisine and if you haven't tried it before, well, there couldn't be a better place to start than Eunice's Terrace.

The casual planting and unassuming appearance of this open-walled two-story building belie the excellent West Indian food one can find inside. Come here for the best conch on the island. Have it cooked in lime juice and butter or fried into a fritter. Or try the old wife (fish) or snapper in a spicy red sauce. Some specials are served only one day a week. If you want to try Eunice's famous souse or salt fish head here Friday; and for kallaloo stew, Saturday is the day. Reservations suggested. No lunch Sunday. *On Smith Bay Road on the east end of St. Thomas. Tel.: 775-3975.*

THE CHILI COOKOFF

If you like chili and happen to be in St. Thomas in late summer check with the Texas Society of the Virgin Islands and see if you're lucky enough to be on island during their annual Chili Cookoff. It's one of the island's great happenings!

Several thousand people show up for this all-day event. The Chili Judges (chili connoisseurs, naturally) rate chili samples for aroma, color, and consistency and take into consideration both the immediate taste and the equally important aftertaste.

Once the judges have had their fill, the general public is welcome to sample as many chili offerings as they can, for a quarter each.

The Chili Cookoff is held on a beach (which one varies year to year). There's live music all day long, and there are all kinds of games and contests – tug-o-war, watermelon seed spitting – to name just a few, and a bunch of prizes. It's a great event and a lot of fun.

TAXIS AND TAXI DRIVERS

Taxis in St. Thomas can range from compact cars that hold just a few passengers to large old station wagons that can accommodate a medium size family plus luggage to vans and open-air safari buses that can carry close to 20.

It is the custom in St. Thomas (and many other islands) to fill up the taxi with people before heading off.

People from the mainland are generally "in a hurry" and can think it's a waste of their vacation time to be made to wait for other people. There is another point of view. Consider, for example, that an islander sees not filling the van as a waste of space (empty seats), a waste of fuel (making the trip twice), and lost income. Plus, what's the hurry?

TAXI TIPS

If you are alone or with one or two others and want to head to your destination immediately, look for a small cab. Drivers of cars that only hold three or four people will be happy to leave immediately.

If you are in Charlotte Amalie and want to go to Havensight, the quickest way is to look for a fairly full van or safari bus where the driver is calling, "Back to the ship." Just hop on and tell the driver you just want to go as far as the Havensight shops.

At hotels, taxis wait in line, and the hotel or doorman will fill taxies with people heading to similar destinations. This can be a good way to meet people and share information.

Don't be shy about taking the front seat next to the driver of your taxi. He or she will be pleased. Do buckle up. It's the law in St. Thomas, and taken very seriously.

If you get a chance, converse with the taxi drivers. They are generally not only kind but very interesting people. Some have lived on St. Thomas for years and can tell you stories about St. Thomas long ago. Many grew up on other Caribbean islands -- Tortola in the BVI, St. Kitts, Antigua, Dominica. You'll also find out that many of the drivers have had numerous careers and lived for long periods in Hartford, Connecticut, or New York City, or Omaha.

If you are planning to get a taxi from the airport, you'll find this is a good time to begin practicing your adjustment to "island time." You'll find that vans sometimes even "wait for the next plane" (which actually won't be that long, since it is probably already on the ground). Hurrying won't get you to your final destination any sooner, and since you have probably already been traveling (including waiting time) from somewhere between four and 17 hours, what's another 15 minutes? Feel and breathe the air and look around.

If you call to have a taxi pick you up, you'll be given the number of the taxi that will come and get you. This number is also the taxi license number so it's easy to know if the taxi headed your way is actually "yours."

The telephone number for the Taxi Lost and Found is 776-8294.

Taxi fares are regulated and the yellow *St. Thomas This Week* prints these fares. The rates in parentheses are for **each** passenger traveling to the same destination. Keep this list with you and agree on the fare with the driver before you leave. Most drivers are honest and helpful but a few do try to take advantage.

THE OLD AIRPORT

Travelers who first headed to St. Thomas before the early '90s remember a completely different airport – rustic perhaps, but chock full of character, and with a long, long walk to the plane. Those who know both airports might enjoy the following story.

AN ISLAND STORY

We have this friend. He lived in New York, but his heart belonged to the Virgin Islands. Several times a year for over two decades the St. Thomas Airport was the gateway to the islands he loved so much.

Each time he de-planed and made that long walk to the WWII hangar that was the terminal building, he made his first stop in what to him was a very special place.

This place had no resemblance to "Rick's" and was unquestionably the opposite of "A Clean Well-Lighted Place." This place was that weary, dark, stale-smelling Sparky's Airport Bar.

Our friend wasn't even much of a drinker, but through the years a cold Sparky's Heineken became almost sacramental. It was the phone booth where his mind slipped out of its three–piece suit and into an island shirt.

Finally, after years of just visiting, he and the wife he loved so much were actually moving — taking up residence in these beautiful islands. A dream come true as they say.

The plane landed at dusk and it was very crowded. The man and his wife entered the terminal from a strange direction. Things seemed different in the airport. Our friend was a little disoriented so he snagged a skycap. "Sorry, how would I get to Sparky's from here?" he asked.

"Sparky's finish, mon. This terminal all new. Progress don't ya know."

Time stopped for a second or two. Then our friend turned to his wife . . . smiled . . . and said, "That's okay. No problem. I wasn't really that thirsty."

He didn't fool her.

--Reprinted from The Best of the Peter Island Morning Sun

SOME GREAT BAKERIES, DELIS, AND TAKE-OUT FOOD

In Charlotte Amalie
Zorba's on Government Hill is a restaurant but they bake bread daily and sell it by the loaf. Stop here for some of the best bread on the island – multigrain, spinach feta, and onion are great and the olive bread is outstanding.

Sub Base (five minutes west of Charlotte Amalie)
Frank's Bake Shop bakes delicious cookies, pies, cakes, tarts, rolls, and breads daily.

Frenchtown
Frenchtown Deli makes great sandwiches (you can create your own or choose from the list on the board), and you can buy cold sodas, a wide variety of beer and ales; cheeses; pates; knockwurst, bratwurst, and andouille sausage; various salads; and freshly-baked breads.

Red Hook
Grateful Deli, across from the American Yacht Harbor complex, has interesting and unusual sandwiches plus a vegetarian menu.

Haagen Dazs Bakery and Ice Cream, also across from the American Yacht Harbor, is hard to pass up if you have any interest in ice cream.

American Yacht Harbor Deli makes excellent traditional sandwiches – ham and cheese, tuna, roast beef.

Marina Market is the best market on St. Thomas and it also has great hot and cold food to go. Come and get a salad or pick up dinner for the whole family. Check out the daily specials.

CHAPTER 5

GREAT WINE BARS, QUIET BARS, & LIVELY BARS

"'Twas a woman who
drove me to drink,
and I never had
the courtesy
to thank her for it."
--*W.C. Fields*

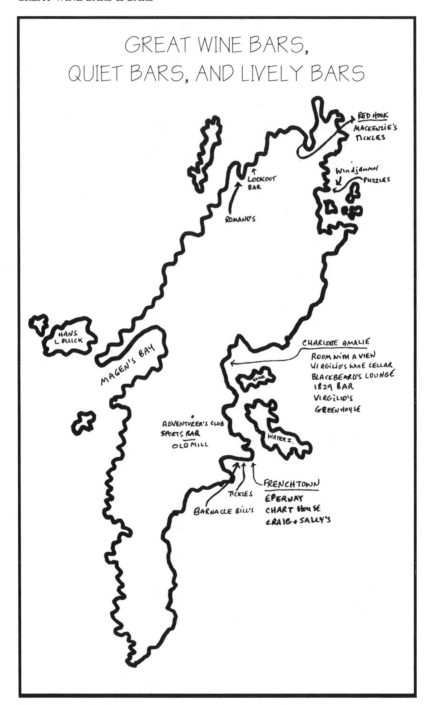

GREAT WINE BARS,
QUIET BARS, AND LIVELY BARS

RED HOOK
MACKENZIE'S
TICKLES

Windjammer
PUZZLES

LOOKOUT
BAR

ROMANO'S

HANS
LOLLICK

CHARLOTTE AMALIE

ROOM WITH A VIEW
VIRGILIO'S WINE CELLAR
BLACKBEARD'S LOUNGE
1829 BAR
VIRGILIO'S
GREENHOUSE

MAGEN'S BAY

WATER I.

ADVENTURER'S CLUB
SPORTS BAR
OLD MILL

FRENCHTOWN
EPERNAY
CHART HOUSE
CRAIG + SALLY'S

TICKLES

BARNACLE BILL'S

GREAT WINE BARS, QUIET BARS, AND LIVELY BARS

St. Thomas has an unusually large assortment of bars of all kinds. There are stylish wine bars (that all also serve spirits), quiet bars in elegant settings, lively and crowded bars, and bars with entertainment and live music.

GREAT WINE BARS

EPERNAY
This is a sophisticated wine bar with a classy decor.

Small tables run along one side of this narrow dark room. Hung from the ceiling are green shades, which hover just above the tables, giving off an intimate glow. There is also a long and comfortable bar. Champagnes and red and white wines of the evening are scrawled on the blackboard, along with the single "Take It or Leave It" entree which changes every night but might be something like chicken with goat cheese, spinach, sun dried tomatoes, and pesto over linguini. There's a long list of cognacs, armagnacs, Spanish brandies, single-malt scotches, and ports by the glass. An appetizer-style menu works for snacks or dinner. You can get a warm spinach salad, a mushroom torte, small seared filet mignon with roasted sweet pepper relish, and goat cheese quesadillas, pate, and Beluga or Sevruga caviar. Closed Sunday. *Frenchtown Mall. Tel.: 774-5348.*

ROOM WITH A VIEW
The decor is swanky 1940s and the view is stunning at this appealing wine bar which looks out over Charlotte Amalie.

A dramatic floor to ceiling window at the far end of the room frames a spectacular view of Charlotte Amalie, the harbor, and the hills beyond. Sunsets here are gorgeous. You can see planes approaching and leaving the airport (the actual runway is hidden by hills) and at night you can watch the planes' headlights and gaze out at the shimmering lights of Charlotte Amalie. The room itself is quite dark, with a little lamp on each table. There's a wine list (by the glass and by the bottle) and a chalkboard by the bar lists daily specials of red wines, white wines, champagnes, and appetizers (such as chocolate covered strawberries). The appealing menu includes a number of appetizers and entrees. You can easily spend an evening here, sampling wines and appetizers and gazing at the stunning view. The mushrooms stuffed with a mushroom, garlic, and cheese mixture, red roasted pepper stuffed with goat cheese, the French Onion soup, and the warmed brie almandine are superb. If you want a full meal, try the excellent tortellini pesto or the shrimp and scallops over pasta or the superbly cooked and very tender West Indian conch. After dinner cordials and specialty coffees and great desserts (Godiva chocolate cheesecake, chocolate sundaes) make this an excellent end-of-the-evening stop if you've already dined elsewhere. Closed Sunday. *Bluebeard's Castle, Bluebeard Hill. 5pm-1am daily. Tel.: 774-2377.*

VIRGILIO'S WINE CELLAR

Head here for the largest wine list on the island, an elegant setting, live piano, cheek-to-cheek dancing, and superb cuisine.

You know you're heading somewhere special when you walk through the entrancing courtyard here, with its waterfalls and clusters of orchids and ferns. Inside dramatic arches, black marble floors, and chandeliers create an elegant atmosphere. Choose a cozy booth or an intimate table or settle in at the long and curvy mahogany bar. There are close to 500 wines in the cellar and 40 to 60 wines are available by the glass. A classical pianist entertains in the evening. The menu includes many small-portion selections in addition to entrees, so you can match your cuisine to your glass of wine. There's a pesto pizza, clams casino, hazelnut crusted fried montrachet on wilted spinach, marinated grilled duck, lobster ravioli, and rack of lamb with porcini mushroom stuffing. Opened by Virgilio Del Mare, of Virgilio's Restaurant fame. Lunch 11:30-3pm, dinner 5pm-1:30am. Closed Sunday. *Charlotte Amalie. Just off of Main Street on Storevater Gade. Tel.: 774-8086.*

FOR GREAT JAZZ . . .
BLACKBEARD'S PIANO LOUNGE

This is the place to come for a great view, a peaceful lounge, and the best light jazz on the island. There's wine and champagne by the glass and a great bar menu that includes desserts. The cold beef tenderloin and the Caesar salad are excellent. Hurricane Marilyn did some damage here but all should be back to normal by the time you are reading this. *Blackbeard's Castle, Blackbeard's Hill.*

GREAT QUIET BARS

Some of the great restaurants on St. Thomas also have small and quiet bars. You can expect to find single-malts, aged ports, and excellent wines and champagnes available by the glass at most of these bars.

CHART HOUSE
You can choose to sit in a rattan love seat or at a table on the terrace that overlooks the harbor. There's also a comfortable bar. *Frenchtown.*

CRAIG AND SALLY'S
This popular Frenchtown restaurant has a dark and comfortable bar with seating on two sides. *Frenchtown.*

1829 BAR
This was originally an old Danish kitchen and the floors and walls are stone and the ceiling is held up with rough-hewn beams. There are backgammon boards here. Check out the blackboard for the daily selection of wines and appetizers. It opens daily at 10am. *Government Hill.*

LOOKOUT BAR
The seats are lined up to give you one of the very best views of St. John and the nearby British Virgin Islands. The sun sets in the opposite direction but sunsets are still beautiful here. If you want to be alone and avoid the crowds waiting for dinner at the popular adjoining Agave Terrace restaurant, walk past the bar to the tiny outside terrace. *Point Pleasant Resort, Smith Bay Road.*

ROMANO'S
This narrow little bar has comfortable seats and you can spend an hour or two reading the labels on all the bottles of grappa and other interesting spirits and wines that line the wall. *East End on Smith Bay Road.*

VIRGILIO'S RESTAURANT
There's a tiny, cozy four-seat bar here. *Storevater Gade, Charlotte Amalie.*

WINDJAMMER
This is a peaceful bar that is never crowded. Cushioned chairs line the long, wide bar. You can eat here, too. Tables ring the room and the best ones are at the far end, looking out to flowers and water. The food is German and the potato soup is particularly delicious. Light meals and hamburgers are also available. Open for lunch and dinner. *Compass Point.*

GREAT LIVELY BARS (AND BARS WITH ENTERTAINMENT)

What's happening when and where changes somewhat, depending on the season. Check St. Thomas This Week *and the Weekend Section in the Thursday edition of the* St. Thomas Daily News *for what is happening when you are on the island.*

ADVENTURER'S CLUB SPORTS BAR

This is a late night spot and doesn't really get going until well into the evening. It's a giant room with a large rectangular bar, booths, pool tables, fooz-ball tables, video games, TVs above the bar, and a big screen television. You can get hamburgers, subs, and pizzas here until 4am 365 days a year. There's a nightclub here, too, which is sometimes open, sometimes not. Check the local papers when you are on island. *Old Mill complex, Contant Hill.*

BARNACLE BILL'S

They lost their landmark rooftop lobster when Hurricane Marilyn blew through but it should be back by the time you are there. Crowds head here to this ultra-casual spot for live music Monday and Wednesday through Saturday. *Sub Base.*

GREENHOUSE

Crowds flock here for dancing to the Starlights every Wednesday and dancing to D.J. music Tuesday and Thursday through Saturday starting at 9. There are sometimes live bands and also specials (like Margarita Monday) or specials surrounding sporting events (like the NBA play-offs). There are pool tables and fooz-ball tables in back. Check the *St. Thomas Daily News* when you are on island for the latest schedules. This is also a restaurant and there are salads, pizzas, pastas, and barbecued ribs and chicken on the menu. *Waterfront Highway in Charlotte Amalie.*

MACKENZIE'S

This lively and popular spot is on the second floor of the American Yacht Harbor complex. There's a large three-sided bar and plenty of tables and people head to this gathering place to meet and mix and watch sports on TV. There's a restaurant here, too, with an early and late night menu of great sandwiches and snacks. *Red Hook.*

OLD MILL

Late night crowds fill this busy nightclub, which is in the first floor of an old mill. There's a D.J. here and Alternative music is featured Thursdays, Generation X music on Fridays. *Old Mill complex on Contant Hill.*

TICKLES

There are two Tickles, one in Red Hook and one at Crown Bay. The latter is a particularly wonderful spot that is busy with local crowds and open to the breezes. Inside is a big rectangular wooden bar that is almost always close to full. But some of the best seats are along the outside of the room, in built-in seats that face outward, open to the breezes and to views of the harbor and nearby Water Island. *Crown Bay Marina.*

THE MOST ORIGINAL BAR

Puzzles wins the prize for the most original bar, certainly on St. Thomas and perhaps anywhere. Your first thought is that you've come across a displaced Mississippi Riverboat but upon closer inspection, well ... it turns out that the owner Jack Rosen salvaged an old glass bottomed boat and turned it into this marvelous bar -- adding everything from the old iron bar chairs to the flowered black carpet to the hundreds of window panes that form the walls.

All kinds of frustrating puzzles are scattered along the bar (like the metal rings that you are supposed to be able to separate without a blow torch). There's a full bar here plus a number of unusual beers on tap and bottled.

If you like sausages, this is the place to come. Bauernwurst, knockwurst, -- whatever he has on hand (he's usually got at least six kinds at any one time), Jack grills and serves with an excellent German potato salad, baked beans, thick chunks of freshly-baked bread, superb mustard, and his non-stop humourous commentary about whatever comes to mind. *Saga Haven.*

"Only Irish coffee provides
in a single glass
all four essential food groups:
alcohol, caffeine, sugar, and fat."
-- *Alex Levine*

ST. CROIX
FOR THE DAY

St. Croix sits by itself about 40 miles south of St. Thomas so it takes a bit longer to get there than it does to get to most of the other neighboring islands. However, you'll still have enough time to have fun on St. Croix, provided you have something specific in mind – you won't have time to do everything.

You can drive around the island and visit several beaches (Budget Car Rental 773-2285), or you can take yourself on an historic walk through downtown Christiansted (directions in the free St. Croix This Week).

You can head out to the Buck Island U.S. National Park (which is different than the Buck Island just off St. Thomas), or you can ride through a rain forest on horseback (call Paul and Jill's Equestrian Stables 772-2880).

You can always take a regular plane, but, at the moment, there are some exciting alternatives. You can travel on a seaplane, a hydrofoil, or a catamaran. Please check to see what is running when you are on island. Over the last 15 years seaplane service and boat transportation between these two islands have come and gone.

BY PLANE
It's a 20- to 30-minute flight, depending on the type of aircraft. Planes leave frequently from the St. Thomas airport. **Dolphin Airlines** (776-9296) heads there six times

a day (round-trip fare is about $86) and **American Eagle** (800-474-4884) flies between St. Thomas and St. Croix several times daily.

BY SEAPLANE
A neat seaplane flies from in front of the Ramada Yacht Haven to in front of the Kings Alley Hotel in Christiansted and it's a quick 17 minutes in the air. There are several morning flights between 6:15am and 11:45am and, for day-trippers, there's a convenient 4:45 return. Fare is $100 roundtrip. Call **Seaborne Seaplane Adventures** at 777-4491.

BY HYDROFOIL
Katran I and **Katran II** are 155-passenger hydrofoils that run between the St. Thomas waterfront (right across from the Windward Passage Hotel) and Gallows Bay on St. Croix. The trip takes an hour and fifteen minutes and is $60 round trip, which includes complimentary soft drinks. (There's also a full bar on board.) If you want a full day on St. Croix, you can catch the 7am or 11:15am boat over and the 5pm boat back. Call **Virgin Island Hydrofoil Services** at 776-7417.

BY CATAMARAN
The **Fast Cat** is a 104-foot long, 124-passenger, wave-piercing catamaran that makes the trip from St. Thomas to downtown St. Croix in about an hour and ten minutes (including docking time). There's an air-conditioned interior and an outdoor deck. Catch it at the waterfront in Charlotte Amalie, across from Vendor's Square. The fare is $50 round trip. For day-trips, there's a 9am departure and a 3:50pm return. Call **Fast Ferries** at 773-3278.

CHAPTER 6

GREAT SHOPPING

"Whoever said money can't buy happiness
didn't know where to shop."

-- Anonymous

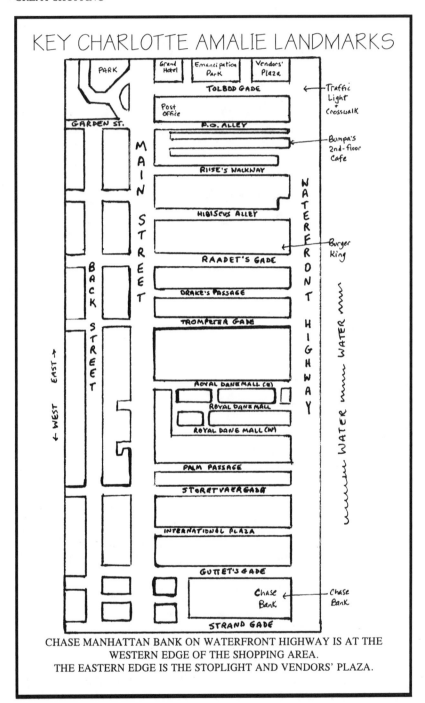

KEY CHARLOTTE AMALIE LANDMARKS

CHASE MANHATTAN BANK ON WATERFRONT HIGHWAY IS AT THE
WESTERN EDGE OF THE SHOPPING AREA.
THE EASTERN EDGE IS THE STOPLIGHT AND VENDORS' PLAZA.

GREAT SHOPPING

Everyone knows that Charlotte Amalie is a world class duty-free shopping mecca, but what no one ever points out is that there are also wonderful, original shops with items you may never find anywhere else tucked here and there in the Charlotte Amalie alleyways and in Red Hook. There are intriguing stores even for people who hate to shop.

SHOPPING IN CHARLOTTE AMALIE
(HAVENSIGHT AND RED HOOK STORES APPEAR AT THE END OF THIS CHAPTER)

Charlotte Amalie certainly gets its share of negative comments. People complain that it's too crowded and full of street hawkers. Well, there are hawkers and it can be very crowded when lots of cruise ships are in. Also, the place itself is confusing, and this is compounded by the throngs of people who make it difficiult to see where you are.

For some people, the crowds are part of the fun. But, if you want to avoid them, head downtown in mid-afternoon. Many cruise ship shoppers will have returned to their ship by then and the town can be quite pleasant. It also helps to go on days when few ships are in.

HOW CHARLOTTE AMALIE IS ORGANIZED
There are two main streets lined with shops: Waterfront Highway and Main Street. Numerous narrow alleys (walkways), also lined with shops, connect these two streets. Each alley has a name (often Danish, with letter combinations non-Danish speaking people find difficult to make sense of). However, you don't really need to know these names because, although you will see these names on maps, a good number of alleys do not have identifying signs.

FINDING YOUR WAY AROUND
So, how do you find anything in this rabbit warren of alleyways with non-pronounceable names that aren't posted? Easy. People rely on landmarks -- just about everything in Charlotte Amalie is either near Burger King, or Chase, or the Post Office. See the map to the left.

CHARLOTTE AMALIE SHOPS

The stores below are selected because they have something special to offer. Most aren't "famous" and some are places that very few people know about. They are organized by category.

Charlotte Amalie's great duty-free stores -- Columbian Emeralds, Sparky's, A.H Riise, Cardow's, and Royal Caribbean (the places where you can buy diamonds and gold jewelry, gemstones, crystal, linens, watches, electronics, perfumes, and cosmetics) -- aren't included below because these renowned shops are covered so thoroughly in virtually every travel book and in free tourist information guides.

BLACK CORAL JEWELRY AND SCULPTURES

BERNARD K. PASSMAN GALLERY
This is a remarkable store and gallery and even people that hate shopping and don't want to browse in an art gallery will probably want to stop and look at these exquisite pieces of jewelry and delicate small sculptures by world-famous Bernard Passman.

There's an exquisite miniature piano made of black coral with all 88 keys and delicate gold pedals and a little black coral stool ($22,000); a miniature drum set complete with cymbals and several miniature drums -- look for the swirls on the drums, which are the natural swirls in the coral ($28,000). There's a delicate image of a Can-Can Girl with 22 Karat gold boots ($175,000). Perhaps the most famous sculpture is that of Charlie Chaplin, with his dog -- in solid gold -- next to him. It's been valued at $1.2 million.

So, what can a regular person afford? There are beautiful gold and black coral bracelets, striking diamond and black coral rings, and lovely pendants in the shape of fish with gold eyes. Prices start at $60 and every single piece is exquisitely detailed and initialed. There's no junk here. There is also no pressure to buy here. The sales people treat the place as an art gallery and are very warm and friendly and will happily explain the history of the more famous pieces even if you are just a browser. *Middle of Riise's Walkway, which is two alleys east of Burger King.*

CARIBBEAN ITEMS

CALYPSO, LTD.

There's a tea and cappuccino bar at the back of this unusual gift shop and you can sample many blends while you consider what to buy. You'll find an eclectic group of items not sold anywhere else on St. Thomas, including many "environmentally-correct" products. There are locally made sauces, jellies from Anegada, jewelry made in St.Thomas and St. John, beautiful jig saw puzzles of Caribbean underwater scenes, gift items made out of recycled paper and natural fibers, shell and wood gift items like big pencils, Caribbean cookbooks, quality children's toys, local spices, skin care products, and coffees and teas. *Inside the A.H.Riise Mall; enter from Main Street -- take the most western entrance and walk through the cosmetics.*

CARIBBEAN PRINT GALLERY

This is a popular spot and also somewhat cramped so if it's too crowded for you just come back later. It's centrally located and easy to get back to. There is a great selection of greeting cards, Caribbean watercolors and paintings, Caribbean maps, beautiful books, and frameable artwork. They have poster tubes for easy traveling. *On Main Street, right in the middle of the A.H. Riise building.*

DOWN ISLAND TRADERS

There is much more to this store than the t-shirts and Caribbean teas, coffees, spices, and jams just inside the entrance -- this is a store that gets better and better the further in you go. Come here for a delightful potpourri of island wares -- Caribbean jams, jellies, and spices, pottery from the St. Thomas Kilnworks, handpainted Christmas tree ornaments, island artwork, watercolor maps of the Caribbean, cards and watercolors by Flukes of the BVI, teas and coffees, greeting cards and cookbooks, beach bags and colorful beach towels, and sterling silver jewelry. And don't forget to look above you. There is lots of great stuff hanging from the ceiling. *The easternmost store in the Waterfront Highway shopping block, at the crosswalk just west of Vendor' Plaza.*

CHOCOLATES AND OTHER GREAT CANDIES

A CHEW OR TWO

This is a chocoholic's super-heaven. You might want to just sniff and savor the Godiva chocolate in the air before getting down to deciding exactly which Godiva truffle you should sample first. It's okay (if you can do it) to go in and just have one. In fact people do this again and again, all day long. If you're

GREAT
ST. THOMAS
SHOPPING FINDS

Cruzan Sterling Silver Bracelets
Godiva Chocolate Truffles
Custom Leather Sandals
The New York Times
Old Virgin Island License Plates
Local Spices and Jams
Leather Luggage
Reggae CDs
Nicole Miller Ties
T-shirts from Local Color
Pusser's Rum & Pusser's Sportswear
Gauzy Dresses
MAPes MONDe Books & Old Maps

stuck, Donna Hodge from Tortola can help you choose from tray after tray of tempting truffles -- double chocolate raspberry truffles, chocolate truffles with Moet & Chandon Champagne or Cognac or Amaretto, French Vanilla truffles with Myers's Rum, or Black Cherry truffles. There are also rum balls, rum cakes, sugar-free chocolates, West Indian jellies, Godiva coffees (hot and by the cup as well as packaged), and gourmet jelly beans (the pear ones are great) which you can buy by flavor or choose your own mix. *On Trompeter Gade, two alleys west of Burger King.*

CLOTHING
(See also Designer Stores)

BACK STREET BOUTIQUE
This great store is just one block back from Main Street and it's a wonderful shop to wander around in; the more you look the more you find.Walls of exposed brick and a quarry tile floor provide an appealing backdrop for an inviting display of clothes and accessories. This is the only St. Thomas store to carry Life Basics clothing -- a California company that makes clothes only out of natural fabrics. Choose from slinky knit t-shirts, linen shirts and short shorts, long slinky skirts, knitted cropped tops, gauzy dresses, handpainted silk scarves, straw hats with flowers and bows, soft blue jeans, and gauzy white cotton jump suits. Colors are soft with lots of whites and off-whites and many shades of soft beige and tan. *Back Street at Storetvaer Gade; see Shopping Map on page 81 for exact location.*

BASE CLOTHING
Base Clothing is a simple but sophisticated line of clothing made in Antigua. This sparsely decorated shop provides a pleasant airy setting for these comfortable, fashionable clothes. There are linen shirts, vests, skinny t-shirts, cropped t-shirts, sarongs, linen dresses, baseball caps, slim pants, and handbags. Colors are soft and earthy -- lots of soft beiges, tans, and browns, plus white and black. *Grand Hotel Complex, east of Post Office.*

COSMOPOLITAN
Come here for Gottex, Bally, Paul & Shark, and Burma Bibas labels. There's a great selection of women's swimwear and swimwear cover-ups. There's also swimwear for men and tennis wear for men and women plus men's slacks, shirts, shorts, and accessories -- including belts and ties. Be sure to check out the upstairs also. *On Waterfront Highway at Drake's Passage, a few stores west of Burger King.*

73

CUCKOO'S NEST

This place doesn't look like much. It's at the end of a dead-end alley and small and a bit crowded inside but it does have good quality and nicely priced linen pants, shorts, and shirts for men. *Drake's Passage, just west of Burger King.*

JANINE'S BOUTIQUE

Stop here for an excellent and ever-changing collection of designer fashion clothing and upscale accessories for women and for men. You'll find selections from Louis Ferand, Cacheral, Christian Dior, Pierre Cardin, YSL, and Valentino. *Palm Passage, three alleys east of Chase Bank.*

KEN DONE

Ken Done is an Australian artist and his brightly colored prints are splashed across t-shirts, beach towels, beach bags, sportswear, bathing suits, and children's clothing. However, there's a lot of great non-Ken Done clothing here, too, including a truly great selection of kids' clothes (head to the back half of the store). *On Waterfront Highway, at Royal Dane Mall.*

LE BADESSE BOUTIQUE

Head here for a selection of great Italian clothes -- Italian swimwear, pants, jackets, shirts and blouses, short skirts, tight mini-skirts and stretch short-shorts, and dressy dresses. *(Taste of Italy complex, on Back Street; see Shopping Map on page 81 for exact location.)*

LOCAL COLOR

Artist Kerry Topper owns this store. She creates the distinctive designs for her line of Local Color T-Shirts. She uses bright primary colors -- reds, yellows, blues -- to create island scenes which are usually framed in a big square. Terry sells her work up and down the Caribbean -- so if you've seen it somewhere else and liked it, head here for a great selection. You can also buy prints of her art that you can hang on the wall. This is also a good place to come for comfortable Jams dresses and shirts and a great selection of hats. There are plenty of clothes for kids here, too. *On Garden Street, north past park across from the Post Office.*

NAME DROPPER

This is one of the best spots on the island for discounted men's and women's designer clothes. There's an equally large variety for men (upstairs) as well as for women (downstairs). For men, you'll find linen and silk shirts and pants, linen shorts, dress clothes, suits, and jackets; for women there are fancy gowns, silk and linen suits and dresses, silk and linen blouses, and a good sportswear collection. Labels include Perry Ellis, Colours by Alexander Julian, Kenar, Jones New York, and Diane Gilman. *On Main Street, at the western edge of town, across from Market Square.*

PUSSER'S COMPANY STORE

If you haven't yet experienced one of the very popular Pusser's Company stores, now is your chance. They are found all over the British Virgin Islands and are one of the best places to shop for comfortable Pusser's sportswear for the whole family. You'll also find a good assortment of island books, appealing souvenirs, and, naturally, the famous Pusser's Rum, available in interesting decanters as well as standard bottles. *On Riise's Walkway; two alleys east of Burger King.*

SOFT TOUCH BOUTIQUE

Shop here for a great selection of classy silk dresses, linen dresses, dressy beaded gowns, silk shirts and blouses, and pants. There are lots of designer labels and also many, many selections in petite sizes. Prices are quite good. *In Grand Hotel Complex.*

COWBOYS AND INDIANS

COWBOYS AND INDIANS

Anyone of any age who likes cowboys and Indians will want to stop in here. A large statue of an Indian greets you as you head up the stairs. Inside you'll find cowboy hats for all size heads, including the tiniest of kids.

There are cowboy vests, cowboy boots, moccasins, belts, and figurines of cowboys and of Indians. There's authentic Indian art from all over the U.S., mugs decorated with Indian art, Pendleton blankets at 30% less than stateside prices, tiles, pottery, and sterling silver jewelry. *Second floor of Grand Hotel Building, which is east of the Post Office.*

DESIGNER CLOTHING

GUCCI
A handsome brick palazzo leads to this cool, peaceful, and elegant store. Here you'll find gracious displays of Gucci ties; Gucci luggage, purses, and wallets; Gucci silk scarves; Gucci shoes for men and women; Gucci coffee cups; and possibly the most expensive t-shirts in the Caribbean. They are Gucci t-shirts, naturally, in bright solid colors, complete with insignia. Of course, you pay the price to show off the insignia -- simple t-shirts are $65, those with collars $85. *Set back from Waterfront Highway near Bumpa's.*

NICOLE MILLER BOUTIQUE
Nicole Miller became famous for her absolutely stunning, delightfully whimsical ties and now, of course, she fashions all manner of things out of these amusing silk prints. They're all available here -- umbrellas, dop kits, address books, boxer shorts, swim suits, bathrobes, vests, and, of course, ties. Come here for a huge selection of her wildly popular and ever-changing collection of ties. Stop here also for Ms. Miller's line of very sexy and feminine dresses -- in solids as well as her famous prints. The 1300 square foot boutique with white marble floor and white stucco arches is a cool classy interior to show off Ms. Miller's sensational silk designs. Stephanie Collins is the manager here and she'll help you find what you want. *On Main Street at Palm Passage.*

GIFTS AND UNUSUAL ITEMS
I FRATI
Come here for a wide assortment of Italian wares -- hand-painted dinnerware, brightly colored papier mache art, napkin rings, silver pitchers and plates, china, blown glass, and various packaged foods. *Back Street in A Taste of Italy.*

LITTLE TREASURES
This is a neat store with an eclectic collection of gift items -- unusual plates, books, clocks, platters, games, and glasswear. The items are nicely arranged and it feels as if someone sorted through a huge amount of merchandise and picked only the unusual and original for an artful display. *On Trompeter Gade.*

SHIPWRECKERS
The unassuming entrance here leads to a delightful surprise. It's a wonderful store to wander about in, whether or not you intend to buy anything. The owner also owns a salvage shop which is how he found much of what you see here. The exposed brick walls are hung with artwork and old maps of the Caribbean,

brilliantly colored live parrots speak their mind, and antique parts of boats are on display (and also for sale). There are beautiful ship wheels and lanterns, plus old coins, maps, and books on the Caribbean. There are even old USVI license plates. There is another branch of this store at Mountaintop. *On the most western Royal Dane Mall alley, four alleys east of Chase.*

LEATHER BAGS & LUGGAGE

THE LEATHER STORE
Step in here, take a deep breath, and savor the smell of expensive leather. This place has a great selection of classy imported handbags, wallets, purses, briefcases, and some luggage. Prices are a lot lower than stateside but still quite expensive. Check out the sale shelves -- usually past the sales counter on the left. There can be truly exceptional bargains here (and at the Havensight branch also). *Main Street, near the Post Office. "Fendi" is on the door.*

PURSES AND THINGS
Walls and tables here are chock full of luggage, purses, briefcases, handbags, and wallets in all sizes and styles and all made of soft and supple Columbian leather. Everything feels so good here and prices are just great! *Two locations: Royal Dane Mall East (west of Burger King) and inside the Hardrock Cafe building.*

MAGAZINES, NEWSPAPERS, AND BOOKS

ISLAND NEWSSTAND
Two walls are jam-packed with all the latest stateside magazines, including *Time*, *Newsweek*, *The New Yorker*, *People*, and *The Atlantic Monthly*. There are also newspapers including *The New York Post*, *The New York Times,* and *The Miami Herald* and hardcovers, paperbacks, and local guide books plus stationery supplies (scotch and packing tape, envelopes, pens, etc.). *On Main Street, a block east of the Post Office. The sign is hard to see so keep looking.*

MUSIC TAPES AND CDs

MUSIC SHOPPE
This is a small spot but the people here are helpful and welcoming. This is a good source for Caribbean music of all kinds including reggae and calypso plus stateside music. There are CDs and cassette tapes and music videos. *On Garden Street, north of the Post Office.*

SHOES AND SANDALS

SHOE TREE
An excellent spot for brand name ladies' shoes. Check out the sale shoes on the floor by the cash register. There's almost always at least one great bargain. They also have a branch at Nisky Center which is located halfway between downtown Charlotte Amalie and the airport. *Off of Waterfront Highway, around the corner from Bumpa's Cafe.*

ZORA'S
Zora's has been here since 1962 and people come from all over the world for custom-made leather sandals that are exquisitely comfortable and last close to forever. There are also ready-made sandals, canvas bags, famous limin' shoes, Great Wall of China backpacks, kids' canvas shark and fish purses, belly bags, and monster backpacks that look, well, just like monsters. If you want custom made sandals, it takes five days so head here on your first or second day of vacation to get measured and to chose a style (there are at least 50, named after places on nearby islands, like Joe's Hill on Tortola). Before you head home you can stop in for a final fitting and to get your sandals. Zora, her daughter, and Ann are caring craftspeople. *A few blocks east of the Post Office, on Main Street. From the Post Office head east over the little hill and look for the stoplight in the distance. The store is on the right, just before the stoplight, where you see a balcony.*

SUNGLASSES AND GLASSES

FASHION EYEWEAR
This is a tiny store and finding it is a good test of your eyes. You'll get great deals on sunglasses here and they can make you prescription glasses in as little as 15 minutes. *From the Post Office head north on Garden Street. You'll see this tiny store right smack in the middle of the road -- actually the road splits in two.*

SWIMWEAR

BEACH HOUSE AT DILLY D'ALLEY
The first floor features appealing resort clothing for women, fancy t-shirts, and numerous accessories, but the real draw is upstairs where you'll find the best selection of women's bathing suits on St. Thomas. The entire second floor

is full of swimsuits of all kinds -- all thoughtfully arranged by style and extremely well-displayed so that it is easy to look through them. There is also a small selection of children's suits.Downstairs there is one small rack of men's bathing suits. *On Trompeter Gade; two blocks west of Burger King.*

TOYS & GAMES

LAND OF OZ
Here's a huge and great collection of toys for people of all ages -- toys that talk and walk and make noises, plus a great assortment of puzzles and games. Keep looking if you don't find something you want right away. The shelves here are packed with great stuff. *Way back in Royal Dane Mall -- look for the little waterfall just in front of the store.*

MINI MOUSE HOUSE TOYS
Don't miss this store even if you have no intention of buying a toy. It's chock full of toys that do things and all of them are turned on! From floor to ceiling toys are in motion -- walking, talking, chirping, and burbling. This is a great place to head if you are feeling down or a tad grumpy. Almost everyone comes out laughing. They also have a great selection of non-noisy toys -- the best on St. Thomas. *Trompeter Gade, south end, and two blocks west of Burger King.*

ANIMAL CRACKERS
This small shop has an interesting collection of childrens' toys and games and also a good selection of kids' clothing. *Sparky's, at Royal Dane Mall.*

FOR A MAP
SHOWING THE LOCATION
OF SHOPS DESCRIBED HERE
JUST TURN THE PAGE.

SHOPS IN CHARLOTTE AMALIE
SEE MAP FOR LOCATION

BLACK CORAL JEWELRY
Bernard K. Passman Gallery-13

CARIBBEAN ITEMS
Calypso-16
Caribbean Print Gallery-15
Down Island Traders-6

CHOCOLATES & CANDIES
A Chew or Two-21

CLOTHING
Back Street Boutique-30
Base Clothing-3
Cosmopolitan-20
Cuckoo's Nest-19
Janine's Boutique-31
Ken Done-26
Le Badesse Boutique-18
Local Color-7
Name Dropper-33
Pusser's Company Store-14
Soft Touch Boutique-4

COWBOY & INDIAN ITEMS
Cowboys and Indians-2

DESIGNER STORES
Gucci-12
Nicole Miller-29

GIFTS & UNUSUAL ITEMS
I Frati-17
Little Treasures-22
Shipwreckers-28

LEATHER BAGS
The Leather Store-10
Purses and Things-32

MAGAZINES, NEWSPAPERS, & BOOKS
Island Newsstand-5

MUSIC TAPES & CDS
Music Shoppe-8

SHOES & SANDALS
Shoe Tree-11
Zora's-1

SUNGLASSES & GLASSES
Fashion Eyewear-9

SWIMWEAR
Beach House at Dilly D'Alley-23
Cosmopolitan-20
Le Badesse Boutique-18

TOYS & GAMES
Animal Crackers-25
Land of Oz-27
Mini Mouse House Toys-24

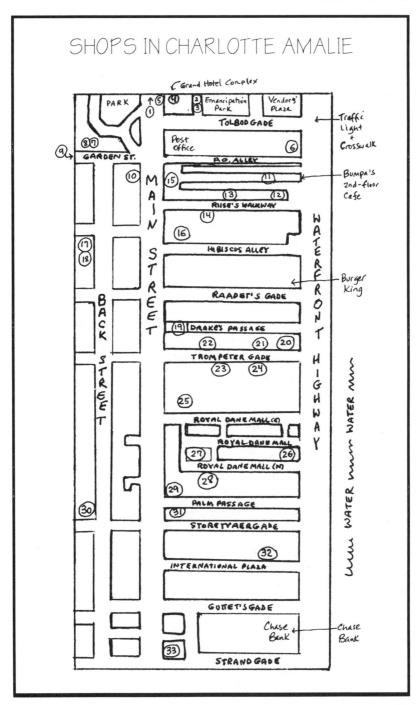

SHOPS IN CHARLOTTE AMALIE

HAVENSIGHT SHOPPING

Havensight was built to make it easy for cruise ship passengers to shop without having to go anywhere. Small branches of many of the duty-free Charlotte Amalie shops are located here in four long one-story buildings that stretch back from the cruise ship dock. It's never really that crowded here and this is an easy place to check out duty-free shops. The absolutely best bookstore in the Virgin Islands is here.

DOCKSIDE BOOKS
Here you'll find two floors loaded with great books of all kinds -- hard cover and soft cover best sellers, shelves and shelves of novels, mysteries, adventures and books on travel, hobbies, cookbooks, and more. Check out the shelf to the left of the cash register for wonderful books that tell about St. Thomas, the Virgin Islands, and the whole Caribbean.

MODERN MUSIC
Directly across the street from Havensight is this great cassette tape and CD store. You'll find the latest stateside releases plus loads of island music. See if you can find a tape by Bankie Banx, a recording star from Anguilla.

RED HOOK SHOPPING

For years, if you were staying on the east end of St. Thomas, you had to "make do" with Red Hook. Yes, you could buy necessities (there was a grocery store and a pharmacy and a gas station) but it was mainly where visitors went to hop a ferry to St. John or the BVI. Now you can shop in the two-story American Yacht Harbor complex. It overlooks a marina and is a pleasant, low-key shopping experience. You'll find several small branches of downtown stores such as Little Switzerland, Sunglass Hut, and La Parfumerie as well as some delightful one-of-a-kind shops.

GREAT STORES IN RED HOOK

BIG PLANET ADVENTURE OUTFITTERS
The cool and dim interior here is a pleasant respite from the hot sun. This is the place to come when you need more Birkenstock sandals, durable Timberland shorts, and practical Patagonia outdoor sportswear. You'll also

find foul weather gear, Jams dresses and sarongs, backpacks, bathing suits, suntan lotion, and sunglasses -- all appealingly displayed.

CHRIS SAWYER DIVING STORE
In addition to diving gear there are bathing suits, sunglasses, hats, sandals, snorkel gear, and a good selection of postcards.

ELIZABETH JAMES
In this appealing jewelry and clothing boutique, quality rather than quantity is the name of the game. There isn't a lot of any one thing but everything here is truly special and nicely displayed. At the back of the store are beaded dresses, washable silk scoop tops, crepe evening slacks, and linen and silk blouses. The front of the store is the showcase for sterling silver and 14k jewelry, much of which is hand-made. This is also the only place besides St. Croix where you can buy the famous Crucian Hook Bracelet that is made in St. Croix. This is also the place to get colorful Bali bird kites.

PUSSER'S WEST INDIES CANDY STORE
Tables here are cluttered with all kinds of delicious candies plus fudges and chocolates and chocolate chip cookies. Plates here and there offer free samples. Don't leave without trying at least one of their fantastic "Good Humor-style" treats -- the chocolate-covered banana or the chocolate-covered wedge of key lime or peanut butter pie are the most popular.

SATORI POTTERY
This is a working pottery studio and an appealing collection of handmade plates, bowls, cups, and more line the shelves. Check upstairs for more items.

ST. THOMAS' BEST MARKET

MARINA MARKET IN RED HOOK
This is absolutely the best market on St. Thomas. Come here for really fresh produce -- red and yellow peppers, portobello mushrooms, yellow tomatoes, numerous lettuces; for excellent wines and champagnes; for specialty items; for a great assortment of upscale stateside brand grocery items; and for a truly great butcher -- place your custom order or choose marinated chicken breasts, small rack of lamb, whole tenderloins, or ground sirloin. Come here also for excellently prepared food to go -- real mashed potatoes, grilled chicken, and a great salad bar. Take it home or eat out on the little terrace.

ART GALLERIES

(MANY GALLERIES WILL SHIP ANYWHERE YOU WANT)

CHARLOTTE AMALIE
THE GALLERY at A Taste of Italy (local artists and photographers, shows change frequently)

UPSTAIRS GALLERY in Palm Passage (works of local artist Jonna White and St. John artist Etre plus tiles, oils, and water colors of other local artists)

CAMILLE PISSARO ART GALLERY (originals and prints by local artists)

CARIBBEAN PRINT GALLERY at A. H. Riise (prints, old maps)

HAVENSIGHT
FREDERICK GALLERY (sculptures, art glass, bronzes, paintings)

AROUND THE ISLAND
TILLET GARDENS at Anna's Retreat (art of all kinds and silk-screened fabrics)

KILNWORKS POTTERY AND ART GALLERY at Smith Bay (pottery plus work by local artists)

MANGO TANGO ART GALLERY at Al Cohen Plaza (Caribbean art, prints, handcrafts)

REICHHOLD CENTER GALLERY at the University of the Virgin Islands (local art)

GREAT THINGS
TO LOOK FOR

THE BIRDS YOU WERE FEEDING LAST SUMMER
Don't be surprised if some of the birds you see look a lot like the songbirds you had in your backyard last summer. They head here from North America every winter, too. Some actually go all the way to South America, stopping here on the way down and on the way back north.

CARS PARKED OVER GUTTERS
In downtown Charlotte Amalie, look for cars parked over deep gutters. How did they get there? Storetvaer Gade, the street Virgilio's restaurant is on, is a good example.

HITCH-HIKING BIRDS
If you take a ferry anywhere, look to see if a bird seems to "hang in the air" close to the boat. It'll be a Brown Booby, hitching a ride. You'll see them actually search out a boat so they can catch a ride in the boat's air wake. If they spot a fish, they'll swoop right down and catch it and then race like crazy to catch back up to the boat to continue their "extra-easy" ride.

HOMEMADE FREIGHTERS
Head down to the Charlotte Amalie waterfront and walk along the harbor until you see some small cargo boats. Stop and read the handmade signs in front of some of the vessels – "Will take cargo to Dominica and Guadaloupe" or "Leaving for Sint Maarten tonight." These small boats travel from island to island, often carrying bananas or other produce north to St. Thomas and bringing freight back to some of the southern islands.

LOCAL
KNOWLEDGE

You can get great deals on certain cosmetics not only while you are on St. Thomas, but even after you return home. Simply call 1-800-289-8784 and order from Luce Caban or anyone else who might answer.

Many of the bricks used in the buildings on St. Thomas were originally used simply as ballast on the ships that came to St. Thomas to pick up cargo. These ships dumped the bricks and filled their hulls with rum and sugar and returned to Europe.

Don't feel stupid if you can't find the store you were in five minutes ago when you are shopping in Charlotte Amalie. This happens to everyone -- including people that have lived on St. Thomas for years.

Some restaurants are closed on Sundays . . . several on Mondays, and a few on Tuesdays. But also the days may change at different times of the year. It's probably best to call first on these days or nights.

You can play DOMINOS every Wednesday and Saturday night at Percy's Bus Stop. If you're interested call Percy at 774-5993.

CHAPTER 7

CHARLOTTE AMALIE LUNCH BREAKS

"Ask not what you can do for your country.
Ask what's for lunch."

--Orson Welles

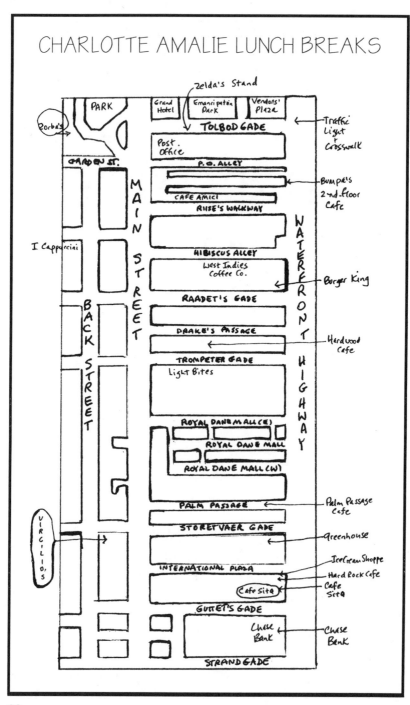

CHARLOTTE AMALIE LUNCH BREAKS

CHARLOTTE AMALIE LUNCH BREAKS

(Where to stop for breakfast, a quick lunch,
a snack, or a cold beverage)

There are many places where you can pause between shops and have breakfast or lunch or a snack or just a cool beverage. These places are generally open from about 7:30am to 4pm. Places that don't serve breakfast open around 11am. See the map for location.

BUMPA'S
This outdoor, second floor cafe is a place to escape the hustle and bustle below. Gaze out at the harbor while you sip coffee and munch on a blueberry muffin or bacon and eggs. Hamburgers and sandwiches are on the lunch menu and the ice cream is great. The puzzle is how do you get up to Bumpa's since there is no visible entrance on Waterfront Highway. Steps are just around the corner.

BURGER KING
A real Burger King -- the menu looks the same, except beer is listed here, and everything tastes just the way it does at a Burger King on the U.S. mainland.

CAFE AMICI
This spot in Riise's Alley offers a peaceful oasis away from the traffic. Umbrellas shade the little marble-top tables which are set on a narrow brick terrace. There's always a soup, quiche, pasta, and sandwich of the day and the menu includes sandwiches, salads, and pastas. The stuffed mushrooms, penne pesto, and grilled eggplant sandwich are delicious. No breakfast.

CAFE SITO
Sit outdoors under an umbrella or indoors in air-conditioned coolness at this inviting restaurant on Waterfront Highway. Try eggplant, sweet peppers, and red onions tossed with linguini or grilled tuna with capers or just have several selections from the tapas menu -- two are usually enough. No breakfast. *For a complete description, see Great Restaurants, page 47.*

GREENHOUSE
This popular Waterfront Highway place is open to the breezes and busy all day long (and actually well into the evening). Come here for a breakfast of Belgian

waffles with strawberries or french toast grilled with bananas. Hamburgers, hot dogs, salads, sandwiches, and pizzas are served at lunch.

HARD ROCK CAFE

Booths and tables sit among rock n' roll decor at this typical Hard Rock Cafe. The moderate-priced menu features chili, cheese nachos, chef salad, California club (a BLT with a grilled marinated chicken breast and swiss cheese), and their incredibly popular "Pig Sandwich" plus burgers, sundaes, banana splits, shakes and malts, and Root Beer Floats. No breakfast.

HARDWOOD CAFE

There are tables outside on Trompeter Gade and a take-out window just next door but the place to eat is inside this cozy air-conditioned restaurant. Tables are close together and it can look too crowded but once you're seated it's okay. Come here for good spinach and caesar salads by themselves or with grilled chicken, quesadillas, stuffed potato skins, hamburgers, stir fry, and pizza.

I CAPPUCCINI

You can eat outdoors or inside at this cozy and casual Italian cafe in the Taste of Italy complex. The short menu includes minestrone and pasta e fagioli soups (both delicious), prosciutto with melon, spaghetti and meatballs, several penne and rigatoni dishes, plus hamburgers and cheeseburgers.

PALM PASSAGE CAFE

People are always walking by (tables here are in the middle of Palm Passage, one of the wider alleys), but it makes for interesting people watching and the food is good. Two nice size bars flank each end of the restaurant and large canvas umbrellas protect the tables from the sun or a passing shower. Come here for good soups, grilled chicken Caesar salad, hamburgers, and sandwiches. There are daily pasta, risotto, and dessert specials.

WEST INDIES' COFFEE COMPANY & EILEEN'S CARIBBEAN COOKIES

It's easy to miss this spot on Hibiscus Alley. The entrance is less than entrancing and you can't tell until you've walked a few steps inside that this is actually a wonderful cappuccino and espresso bar. Daily specials are on the blackboard and there are numerous baked goods to choose from.

ZORBA'S

In back of Cafe Sagapo, on Government Hill, is this casual outdoor terrace that seems a million miles from the bustle of downtown Charlotte Amalie.

Food is exceptional here. There are sandwiches on delicious homemade bread, gourmet pizzas baked in a wood oven, and Greek specialties like spinach pie, hummos, and eggplant salad. *For a complete description, see Great Restaurants, page 48.*

VIRGILIO'S -- FOR A RELAXING ESCAPE

For some of the best Italian food anywhere, in a sophisticated setting that seems a world away from the crowded streets of Charlotte Amalie, step into Virgilio's on Storetvaer Gade. Soft lighting and polished service provide the perfect backdrop for a glass of champagne, a salad, and freshly grilled fish or the pasta of the day. Reservations are a good idea (776-4920). *For a complete description, see Great Restaurants, page 42.*

SNACKS AND ICE CREAM

ICE CREAM SHOPPE
This may not look like much but this tiny take-away place has delicious ice cream cones, yogurt, and hot dogs plus West Indian snacks like fish fry, johnnie cakes, chicken soup, and meat pates. It's tucked into a corner next to the Hard Rock Cafe souvenir store.

LIGHT BITES
This place is very casual but the food is fresh and the tables are quiet. You can get food to go or sit at inside tables. There are daily specials like spaghetti and meatballs plus fresh salads, pasta salads, sandwiches, and quiches. It's on Trompeter Gade.

ZELDA'S STAND
When you're ready for a bottle of ice-cold water or a cold, cold soda head to this little stand. It's on Tolbod Gade, between the Post Office and the Hospitality Center (across from Vendor's Plaza). There's no sign so look for a pretty lady who's wearing a colorful wide-brimmed bonnet and a beautiful smile. Her stand is simply a little silver cart and a cooler but she's got icy cold sodas, bottled water, and juices plus candy, sugar cakes, chips, and little bags of peanuts. And she can see the good side of just about everything.

ALWAYS . . .

Always be nicer to people than necessary.

Always lock your hotel room and rental car.

Always have a hat, bandanna, or something to cover your head during the day.

Always remember to keep left when you are driving.

Always look right, first, and then left before crossing the street.

Always put on some sun screen before going outside during the day.

Always greet people before conducting any "business."

Always remember the sometimes slower pace you encounter is part of St. Thomas' charm.

Always snorkel with at least one other person.

ST. JOHN FOR THE EVENING

Many visitors to St. Thomas never realize how incredibly easy it is to head over to St. John just for dinner. In fact, if you are staying on the east end of St. Thomas it is possible to go to St. John for dinner in about the same length of time that it would take you to get to downtown Charlotte Amalie.

Most of the ferries have an uncovered upper level and you can ride over basking in the afternoon sun and return at night in a seat open to the soft Caribbean breezes and under a blanket of stars and perhaps a full moon.

Getting there on a ferry.
The ferry dock is right in the middle of the east end of St. Thomas, at Red Hook. Ferries run hourly from Red Hook to Cruz Bay on St. John and the ride takes less than 20 minutes. Get there a little early if you want to be sure to get a seat up top. The fare is $3 and the ferry takes you to the dock right in the heart of Cruz Bay, which is St. John's only real town. It's a little tiny town and very different from anything on St. Thomas.

Getting to St. John by Water Taxi.
If you prefer a private ride, **Per Dohm Water Taxi** will take you over to St. John in one of their power catamarans in a quick 15 minutes. They'll come back and pick you up whenever you have finished dinner (they only need 15

minutes notice -- and someone at the restaurant will usually be kind enough to call while you are settling the check). If there are four of you this turns out to be a little more than twice the cost of the public ferry.

Is there somewhere great to watch the sunset?
If you plan on eating early, the terrace at Asolare faces out over the water toward the setting sun. If you'd prefer to see the sunset with a beverage before dinner, head to the third floor bar at **Ellington's** at Gallow's Point Resort (a five-minute walk from the ferry dock). Seats here are arranged to catch the best view.

Are the chances of catching the "green flash" good?
It's extra-hard to catch the "flash" because of all the little islands in the way but there are a few times during the year when you can actually see the sun slip into the water between the islands and then your chances are pretty good.

What are some good restaurants on St. John?
Two of the best are **Asolare** (several minutes by cab) for a spectacular view and fine cuisine with an intriguing eastern touch and **Paradiso**, with a menu of grilled fish and steak and pastas. It's in Mongoose Junction (a five minute walk from the ferry dock) as is the more casual **Mongoose Restaurant**.

Other excellent choices are waterfront **Seychelles** for gin shrimp, good bouillabaisse, and an assortment of pastas; **Pusser's** for good steaks; and the **Fish Trap**, which has terrific fish in an informal setting. If you have time stop by the **Bad Art Bar** and check out the ceiling.

Note: Ferries leave Cruz Bay on the hour until 10pm. One more ferry -- the very last one -- leaves Cruz Bay at 11:15pm. If you miss this, well,...you're on St. John for the night.

CHAPTER 8

GREAT WATERSPORTS & BEACHES

"Babies don't need a vacation, but
I still see them at the beach."
--*Steven Wright*

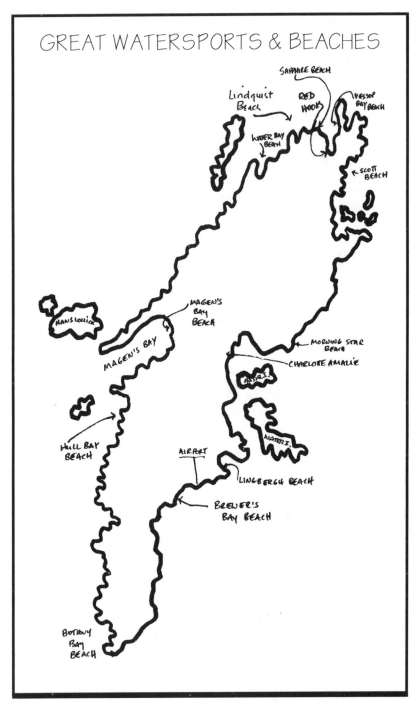

GREAT WATERSPORTS & BEACHES

GREAT WATERSPORTS

St. Thomas offers practically every watersport imaginable. You can snorkel off the edge of a beach, take out a sunfish, go for a sail, scuba dive day or night, try your hand at parasailing, hop onto a jet ski or a wave runner, paddle a kayak, or pedal a pedal boat. You can also rent a little power boat or charter a boat and visit beaches on other islands (see pages 120 and 123). St. Thomas is also a particularly good place to try one of these activities for the first time. Watersports centers here, more so than on most islands, really do specialize in teaching the beginner as well as outfitting the expert.

JET SKIS AND WAVERUNNERS
Skim over the waves at many locations. On Lindberg Bay, call **Mad Max** at 775-5178. If you are in East End or Charlotte Amalie call **Caribbean Watersports** at 775-4206.

KAYAKING
In the Virgin Islands, there are actually two kinds of kayaking. Many resorts have brightly colored one- and two-person "kayaks" which are fun to take out. You can have races or just paddle about. The kayaking sport is also popular in the Virgin Islands. You can rent real kayaks and join kayaking trips. Call **West Indies Wind Surfing** at Vessup Bay Beach (775-6530) and see page 123.

PARASAILING
Want to take a ride 500 feet above the water? This popular sport is easy to do. You don't even have to get wet. You're strapped into a parachute, a speed boat surges forward, and up you go! Boats leave from many locations. Call **Caribbean Para-sailing** (777-3055) or **Caribbean Watersports** (775-4206).

PEDAL BOATS
Quite a few St. Thomas resorts have these little contraptions. They look sort of silly but once you're in one, they can be fun. Basically two people sit in a floating set of chairs and pedal around -- the faster you pedal the faster you go. It's interesting to look back at the shore and a slow trip takes almost no energy. Bring a soda or a pina colada.

SNORKELING

Snorkeling equipment (mask, fins, snorkel) is available at virtually all resorts on St. Thomas and can be rented on many beaches. The water is clear here and you will see many colorful little fish. First-timers may want to try snorkeling right off the beach -- although you won't see a lot of fish it's still interesting to look around and see what's going on down there and you can practice breathing -- slow and steady is the key. If you want to go on a snorkeling trip (there are many to choose from) call the **Charterboat Center** (775-7990) and they'll match you with the trip that is right for you.

SCUBA DIVING

St. Thomas is surrounded by lots of good diving sites. If you've always wanted to try diving now is a good time. It's possible to take a resort course and actually dive the same day. **Chris Sawyer Diving Center**, with locations at Red Hook (777-7804), the Renaissance Grand Beach (775-1510, ext 7850), and Compass Point Marina (775-7320), is one of the best.

WINDSURFING

Lots of people spend hours trying to stay on these things. If you don't feel like trying it yourself, do find a good spot on the beach where you can watch someone else try. It's often very funny. Most resorts rent windsurfing equipment and also give lessons. If you want to windsurf and can't where you are staying then ask at reception which would be the closest place for you to go.

> "There's nothing quite like getting out
> on the open sea, where you can forget
> about the hassles and worries
> of life on land, and concentrate
> on the hassles and worries
> of life on the sea."
>
> *-- Dave Barry*

GREAT BEACHES

St. Thomas has many great beaches. Some are undeveloped. Others are in front of resorts. Year after year long and stunning Magen's Bay Beach is voted one of the world's ten most beautiful beaches. Magen's Bay Beach was donated to St. Thomas by Arthur S. Fairchild in 1946 (along with 45 adjoining acres) to be preserved forever as a public park. On St. Thomas, as in all of the USVI, all beaches are open to everyone, even if there's a resort there.

Bear in mind that a beach in front of a resort is "groomed" at least once or twice a day. Workers pick up trash, rake the sand, and clip and water the tropical foliage that borders the beach. Anyone used to a "groomed" beach can think a natural beach in the Caribbean looks "messy" -- but it's not really. It's just that there's no one around to remove the seaweed, or pick up the detritus the waves have tossed on shore.

BOTANY BAY BEACH is way out at the western tip of the island. It's a long drive and a bit of a walk but the snorkeling is very good here.

BREWER'S BAY BEACH is west of the airport (keep the airport on the left as you drive west on Brewer's Bay Drive - Rte 30). You'll find the beach after you drive all the way through the campus of the University of the Virgin Islands. This is a nice beach for swimming and walking along and there are several snack trucks parked there daily. This beach is close to the final approach to the St. Thomas airport and is a great place to watch planes of all sizes come in for a landing.

HULL BAY BEACH is on the north shore and you'll see lots of little painted fishing boats bouncing at their buoys. It's not a great swimming beach mostly because there are so many little boats in the water. Larry's Hideaway Bar and Grill, which is a bit behind the beach, is a popular barefoot bar that often has entertainment on weekends. The menu ranges from hot dogs to chicken sandwiches to linguini with meat sauce.

LINDBERGH BEACH is practically across the street from the airport and it's a nice long beach for walking and is also a calm swimming beach. Not very many large planes fly in and out of St. Thomas so the airport noise really isn't a problem. There are several hotels here, including the Island Beachcomber.

You can rent jet skis and wave runners and go waterskiing here. There's also some fine food to be had at the little snack bar wagons parked along the road.

LINDQUIST BEACH (aka Smith Bay Beach) is on the eastern shore and it's one of the few easily-accessible beaches that is still completely undeveloped (although plans threaten to change this). The swimming here is excellent. This is a nice long beach lined with sea grapes. It's great for walking and taking in the views of Thatch Cay and Grass Cay. On Smith Bay Road (between the entrance to Pavilions and Pools and the Wyndham Sugar Bay) are two dirt roads just yards from each other that lead to this beach. One is about a minute north of Pavilions and Pools, is quite bumpy, and can involve encounters with big cows. The less bumpy, easier (no cows) dirt road is just a few yards further on and two signs make it easy to spot -- coming from Red Hook look for the green airport sign. If you're heading to Red Hook, turn left at the 35mph sign.

MAGEN'S BAY BEACH, on the north shore of St. Thomas, is one of the most beautiful beaches in the world but it is also quite popular. Arthur S. Fairchild donated Magen's Bay and 45 adjoining acres to St. Thomas in 1946. The beach is a very long gentle curve of dazzling white sand and the water is exceptionally calm. There's $1 per vehicle and $1 per person entrance fee and you can rent beach chairs, floats, towels, snorkeling equipment, and lockers. There's a cafeteria-style snack bar and a large beachwear shop.

MORNING STAR BEACH is just outside of St. Thomas harbor. Marriott's Frenchman's Reef and Morning Star Resorts are here and there are several restaurants and bars along the beach. You can rent beach chairs and snorkel equipment and take windsurfing and sunfish lessons. The beach is fairly long and generally calm for swimming, although it can have a little swell.

SAPPHIRE BEACH RESORT BEACH is on the east end of St. Thomas and it's an active beach. You can parasail from here, rent waverunners and sunfish, take windsurfing and scuba diving lessons, and rent floats and beach chairs.

SCOTT BEACH is at the southeastern end of the island near Compass Point. You can rent beach lounges and umbrellas.

VESSUP BAY BEACH is a quiet beach that usually is calm for swimming. It's near Cabrita Point and across from the American Yacht Harbor complex.

WATER BAY BEACH (where the Renaissance Grand Beach Resort is located) is a 1000-foot long beach with lots going on. You can rent jet skis, sailboats, pedal boats, windsurfers, sunfish, and waverunners.

GOLF, TENNIS, & FITNESS CENTERS

GOLF

George and Tom Fazio designed this championship 18-hole golf course at **Mahogany Run** on the north side of the island. It's particularly famous for its 13th and 14th greens that sit atop a cliff high above the Atlantic.

FITNESS CENTERS

When you feel the need for a workout, the following places have weight machines, free weights, treadmills, stairclimbers, bicycles, and even personal trainers.

Carib Health Complex at Sub Base (774-4472)
Club Elysian Fitness Center at Bolongo Elysian Beach Resort (775-1000)
Gold's Gym (yes, just like in the states) next to the Hard Rock Cafe in Charlotte Amalie (777-9474)

TENNIS

Marriott's Frenchman's Reef, Renaissance Grand Beach Resort, and **Wyndham Sugar Bay** each have at least four courts and most other resorts have a court or two.

A FULL DAY
IN PARADISE

A breakfast in bed or on a beach
A morning stroll and a swim
A few pages under the palms
maybe a massage
A junket to St. John with lunch in
Cruz Bay
A dessert or two by the dock
A soft drink for the voyage back
Another swim, a nap, a bubble bath
A cocktail under the stars
A romantic repast for two
A barefoot dance in the breezes
A port on the porch. . . and
then to bed.

CHAPTER 9

GREAT ISLAND ATTRACTIONS

"There are more than ninety-nine steps
to these ninety-nine steps."

-- Peter P., age 9
from Visiting the Virgin Islands with the Kids

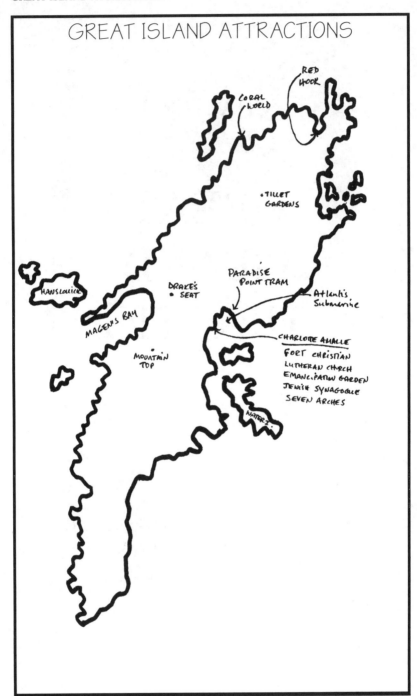

HISTORICAL SIGHTS

There is much more to Charlotte Amalie than shopping. The town is listed in the National Register of Historic Places for its history and for its architecture. Below are descriptions of some of the most interesting buildings. If you want more information, you can find a nice selection of books and pamphlets (including an excellent walking tour) for sale in the Virgin Islands Museum shop at Fort Christian.

FORT CHRISTIAN

They've been restoring this National Historic Landmark for what seems like forever and there's still more to do. However, some exhibits are open. It's the earliest known building in town and was probably started around 1666. You can learn about famous local people, see examples of furniture that was typically in homes here 100 years ago, check out exhibits of shells, local fauna and flora, and birds. Changing exhibits by local school children focus on such things as protecting the environment and being kind to animals. There's a small room devoted to Arona Peterson's remarkable drawings of medicinal plants. *Waterfront Highway (entrance around back).*

FREDERICK EVANGELICAL LUTHERAN CHURCH

This church was established here in 1666 and the present building was started in 1789. A wide yellow brick stairway leads up to the arched entranceway. The ceiling of the church is dramatically arched and the wood in the chancel and pulpit is local mahogany. *Free. On Main Street, two blocks east of the Post Office.*

EMANCIPATION GARDEN

This is the park right in front of the Grand Hotel complex and is dedicated to the emancipation of the slaves in the Danish West Indies on July 3, 1848. Many local celebrations and events are held here. *Grand Hotel complex.*

JEWISH SYNAGOGUE

Founded in 1796, this is the oldest Hebrew house of worship in continuous use under the U.S. flag. The benches and ark are fashioned out of local mahogany. The floor is sand, symbolic of a time when Jews in Spain were forced to practice their religion in secrecy and did so in cellars, using sand to muffle the sound. The walls here are bricks held together by sand, limestone, and molasses and it is said that years earlier children used to lick the walls to get a taste of the sweet molasses. *Donations accepted. Crystal Gade.*

SEVEN ARCHES MUSEUM

Ring the bell at the black iron gate and someone will let you in to this restored private house, built with yellow ballast bricks from Denmark. Take a look at the stone oven in the original Danish kitchen. This is what people used to cook everything in, from stews and roasts to loaves of bread. Kids of all ages will like climbing up the steps to the high porch and seeing the many iguanas roaming about. *Small donation requested. Follow Main Street up over the hill past the Government House and look for a little sign on the left and follow the sign halfway down the alley.*

ATTRACTIONS AROUND THE ISLAND

St. Thomas has a number of "tourist attractions" but some of them really are quite special. They are popular stops on the cruise ship crowd circuit, but you can see them all without the throngs if you head there early morning or late afternoon. Early, early morning is a great time to catch the views and take stunning photographs at places that are always open, like Drake's Seat.

CORAL WORLD

Call to see if Coral World is open. It was one of the great St. Thomas attractions until Hurricane Marilyn blew it apart, but it's being rebuilt and is supposed to open in early 1997. The advertising can make it look too "touristy" but what you see here is great. So, what do you see? A "Touch Pond" with all kinds of sea creatures including some weird ones -- a sea cucumber that spits, a worm that goes inside itself when you touch it. The Underwater Observatory lets you look right into the ocean. Circular stairs lead down into an underwater room ringed with windows that look out into the water. You see the surface up above and all kinds of fish and underwater plants and corals all in their natural habitat. It's like snorkeling without getting wet. You can see live lobsters hiding in the rocks, shimmering silvery waves of giant schools of tiny fish moving as one, and fish hovering just outside the window, gawking at you.

In the Marine Gardens Aquarium are spectacular little seahorses and sea life that glows in the dark. Shows include shark feedings and fish feeding but the absolute all-time best is the Bird Show -- birds ride bicycles, walk a tightrope, play basketball, and roller-skate. Coral World is definitely worth a visit. If you hate crowds, go towards the end of the day. You'll miss the shows but you'll be almost alone. *Coki Point.*

ATLANTIS SUBMARINE

Hop into this air-conditioned, 46-passenger submarine for a mile and a half-long underwater tour through the underwater National Wildlife Preserves of Buck Island, just outside of St. Thomas harbor. The sub descends to 90 feet and wide windows in front of every seat give you a good look at hundreds of colorful tropical fish and numerous kinds of coral. The excursion takes two hours (but you are underwater for only 50 minutes) and dives leave hourly 9am to 3pm Monday through Saturday. *Cruise ship dock at Havensight.*

MOUNTAIN TOP

Come here 1547 feet above sea level for a stunning view overlooking St. Thomas and Magen's Bay and the British Virgin Islands. There's a little restaurant, a number of shops, and a long viewing terrace. Bring your camera. *Off of Route 33.*

DRAKE'S SEAT

Legend has it that Sir Francis Drake used this spot as a lookout to spot enemy Spanish fleets. It's just a parking area with a truly spectacular view of Magen's Bay. Vendors are here during cruise ship hours and there is a donkey decked out in bougainvillaea blossoms that kids can have their picture taken with. Come here early morning or late afternoon to be alone and just absorb the view. *Route 40.*

PARADISE POINT TRAM

Swiss-built gondolas carry you up 700 feet to the top of Flagg Hill and a spectacular view of Charlotte Amalie and the harbor. The trip takes five minutes and stores and a restaurant and bar await you. The outdoor terrace is a perfect place to relax and take in the view. *Across from Havensight.*

RENTING WHEELS

Car rentals can be arranged through most hotels. **Avis** (800-331-1084, 809-774-1468), **Budget** (800-527-0700, 809-776-5774), and **Hertz** (800-654-3131, 809-774-1879) all have locations at the airport and Budget also has four other locations around the island. **Dependable Car Rental** (800-522-3076, 809-774-2253) is a caring family-owned operation that provides excellent and reliable service.

TILLET GARDENS ART CENTER

Stone walkways, shaded by a canopy of spreading tree tops, meander lazily through small gardens at this remarkable and peaceful collection of art galleries and working artist studios.

There is an art gallery, an enamel guild, a goldsmith, a silk-screening studio, a stained glass studio, a hand-painted porcelain and doll workshop, and a Caribbean crafts gallery. When you are ready for a break, stop in at Polli's for a margarita or a meal. It's a good Mexican restaurant.

Internationally acclaimed artists from around the world perform at Classics in the Garden, a series of four Wednesday night concerts held during the winter season.

Arts Alive, a once-a-year event, is held every fall and is a showcase for local artists, sculptors, and designers.

CHAPTER 10

LITTLE
ST. JAMES
ISLAND

"If one morning I awake and discover
my name on the Forbes list of the
400 Richest People in the U.S.,
I shall travel immediately
to Little St. James Island."

-- H. H. Hankshaw III

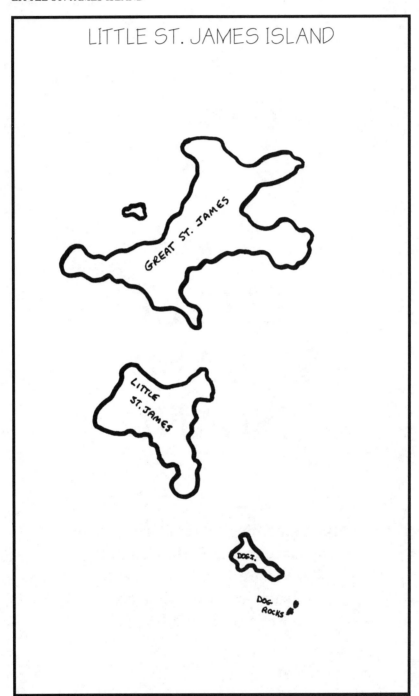

LITTLE ST. JAMES ISLAND

When nothing less than a private island will do, just head over to luxurious Little St. James Island for a week or so. This 72-acre private island lies just off the eastern shore of St. Thomas.

A luxurious Great House and four separate sleeping pavilions await you. In the Great House is an expansive and elegant living room with comfortable seating areas arranged here and there to catch the best views. There's also a library and video room and kitchen. Each detached sleeping pavilion has an antique four-poster bed and its own spacious private bath and dressing area.

All along the walls of the Great House and the sleeping pavilions are tall and slender louvered doors that show off stunning views of neighboring islands and the blue, blue Caribbean water. Walls are fashioned from Mexican coral stone. Floors are partridgewood from South America. Furnishings are primarily European and West Indian antiques. There's an extensive wine selection, kept, of course, in the temperature-controlled wine cellar.

Outdoor pleasures include a large oval pool plus three beaches, acres of hiking trails, and great snorkeling spots. Sea kayaks, sailboards, fishing equipment, and a 27-foot motorboat are yours if you want.

And what about service? Well, the staff includes a full-time gourmet chef, housekeeper, boatman, gardeners, and a caretaker. And the price? Two of you can have it for just $16,500 a week, which includes boat or helicopter service between St. Thomas and Little St. James, meals, beverages, and just about everything else. *Call McLaughlin Anderson at 1-800-537-6246.*

Some Helpful Hints

DRIVING AROUND THE ISLAND
St. Thomas is an island of spectacularly steep hills and the views up top are simply stunning. It's definitely worth it to take a drive around the island. It's nice to have the freedom of a car, but consider taking a taxi tour first -- to get your bearings, to get a sense of local driving habits and the steepness of the roads, and to be able to concentrate on the scenery instead of the curves.

WHAT, NO ELECTRICITY?
Don't worry when the electricity suddenly goes off. It happens all the time and it's no big deal. (That's why you have a candle in your hotel room.) You don't even have to be very patient as the power almost always comes right back on just a few minutes later.

INVISIBLE BUGS WITH A BITE
At sundown, especially when it is not windy, annoying little 'no-see-ums' appear out of nowhere and bite. Insect repellant generally keeps them at bay and wind keeps them away. For some people, these bites have a lasting itch and it's good to have a medication like Sting-Eze around. A dab of gin will work in a pinch.

FERRY BOATS TO OTHER ISLANDS
Ferries for St. John and the British Virgin Islands leave from Red Hook and the waterfront at Charlotte Amalie. Ferries to St. Croix only leave from the Charlotte Amalie waterfront.

WATER AND HASSEL ISLANDS

WATER ISLAND
A quarter-mile off the south shore of St. Thomas lies Water Island, a hilly little island with a curvaceous shoreline. It has a pretty little sweep of a beach known as Honeymoon Beach and one very casual and very little hotel. There are private residences here but there is not one single restaurant or store on the island.

A DAYTIME BEACH ADVENTURE
For a little daytime beach adventure, head over to Crown Bay Marina and catch the little ferry to Water Island. To spend the morning or the afternoon you'll probably want to catch the 8am, 11am, noon, or 2pm ferry. (You can get an 11:30am, 12:30pm, 2:30pm, and 4:30 pm ferry back. The fare is $3 per person each way.) You'll see the little boat alongside the dock in front of Tickles Restaurant and Bar at Crown Bay Marina. Just hop on and wait. The pilot will show up soon enough (he's usually off getting supplies for the island).

The trip takes five minutes. There are absolutely no facilities here so you'll need to bring everything you might want to have with you – towels, sun screen, a cooler with water and sodas, and perhaps lunch.

GETTING AWAY FROM IT ALL FOR A WEEK OR TWO
If you really want to get away from everything and are content with comfortable but basic furnishings, you might want to stay on Water Island at the **Limestone Reef Terraces**, a little group of ten motel-like efficiencies on a hill with great views. There's not much to do except

sit around and read and look at the views. Or take a walk or head down to one of the beaches. (Honeymoon beach is the swimming beach. A coral beach on the other side of the island is good for snorkeling.) Or occasionally take the ferry to town for supplies.

By the way, you're not completely isolated if you are staying here, since you can take a boat back to the marina where there's a restaurant and stores. The ferry will also drop you at Charlotte Amalie during the day. For an additional fee, it will also take you there and back in the evening. Randy is the manager of **Limestone Reef Terraces** (800-872-8784, 809-774-2148), the handyman for most of the island, and the sole taxi driver. He can take you to hilltops with great views of nearby and uninhabited Savana and Saba Islands. There's also a three bedroom house for rent on Catchment Hill, where you can actually see all the way to Puerto Rico.

HASSEL ISLAND
This is the island that sits right in the middle of St. Thomas harbor. Although there are a few private residences, most of the 135-acre island is part of the Virgin Islands National Park. Trails have not been maintained but if you want a bit of a rugged hike, it is possible to follow them. The National Register of Historic Places lists four spots on this island, including an old coal mining station and shipyard. These are unrestored and pretty much in ruin at the moment. Occasionally there are guided hikes. Call 775-6238 for information.

So how do you get here? Try Larry's Launch in Charlotte Amalie or check with "The Reefer" ferry that runs between downtown Charlotte Amalie and Marriott's Frenchman's Reef Hotel. Sometimes they will drop you off and pick you up.

CHAPTER 11

THE BRITISH VIRGIN ISLANDS FOR A DAY

"I never met a place like this in my life."
-- Hugh Benjamin

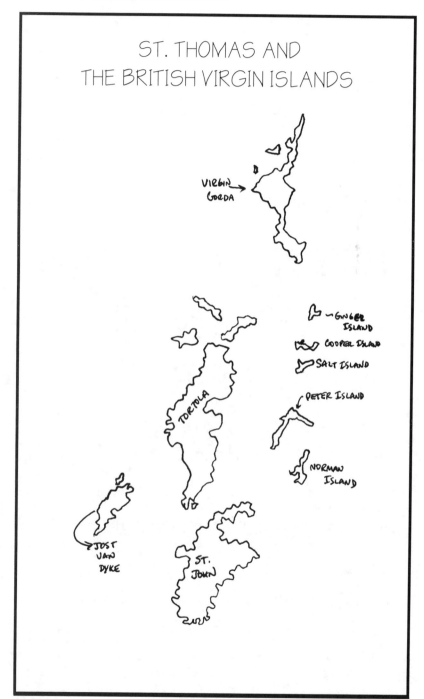

ST. THOMAS AND THE BRITISH VIRGIN ISLANDS

VIRGIN GORDA

GINGER ISLAND

COOPER ISLAND

SALT ISLAND

PETER ISLAND

NORMAN ISLAND

TORTOLA

JOST VAN DYKE

ST. JOHN

THE BRITISH VIRGIN ISLANDS FOR A DAY

One of the great things about staying on St. Thomas is that it is so incredibly easy to drop over to the British Virgin Islands for a day. It's hard to imagine how close these islands are until you get to the east end of St. Thomas and see that you can practically swim to them. Though the BVI look very similar to the USVI -- green and remarkably hilly, you'll find that in character they are astonishingly different. You will definitely feel that you have visited another country -- and perhaps even another era.

Because the BVI are a remarkably tight cluster of mountainous islands, they are easily viewed from the air or the sea. You can fly over all of them in less than an hour. Or you can choose one of several excellent boat trips that cruise through the islands, stopping for snorkeling excursions and a walk through the famous Baths on Virgin Gorda. Or you can rent a small power boat and do your own piloting and take yourself wherever you wish.

THE BVI FROM THE AIR

One of the quickest and most spectacular ways to get an overview of the BVI is to simply fly over them. It takes less than an hour and the views of the land and the water are stunning -- emerald green hills you can almost reach out and touch, crescent white sand beaches, and water in an unbelievable number of brilliant neon blues.

SEABORNE SEAPLANE ADVENTURES (777-4491) offers a ninety minute, narrated "flightseeing" tour (45 minutes of flight time) that flies over all the U.S. and British Virgins, including far away Anegada. Double-size windows show off outstanding views and you get to take off from the water, a thrill in itself. Catch it at the Ramada Hotel Marina, between downtown Charlotte Amalie and the cruise ship dock. (Seaborne's office is in the hotel courtyard.) Tours are $79 per person and offered several times daily from 9am to 4pm.

AIR CENTER HELICOPTERS (775-7335) takes two to six people on a 25 minute sight-seeing flight over Jost Van Dyke and Tortola. Cost is $110 per person, minimum two people. You can also design your own tour. Helicopters leave from the waterfront's west end in Charlotte Amalie across from the Windward Passage Hotel. Closed Sunday.

HILL AVIATION (776-7880) takes one to six passengers on a 30 minute helicopter tour of Tortola. The cost is $330 for one or two people, and $110 for each additional person. You can also charter the helicopter for $660 an hour, take up to six people, and choose your own route. Helicopters leave from Frenchman's Reef Hotel, ten minutes east of Charlotte Amalie.

THE BVI FROM THE WATER

When you are staying on St. Thomas, two of the best ways to sample the British Virgin Islands by sea are by joining a group for an all-day power boat trip or renting your own small boat. Both options are available from the east end of St. Thomas. You absolutely must have proof of citizenship (voter's registration card, birth certificate with raised seal, or passport).

GROUP BOAT TRIPS

There are advantages to going with a group on a large power boat. Power boats are the only boats with enough speed to easily reach many British Virgin Islands in a day, so you get to see almost all the islands from the water, and you get to actually visit several islands. You are taken directly to excellent snorkeling areas and an expert goes in the water with you.

What to bring: soft-soled shoes, camera and plenty of film, a swimsuit and towel (it's easy to change on board), non-oily sun screen, and proof of citizenship. If you have a prescription snorkel mask, don't forget it!

LIMNOS CHARTERS (775-3203), which leaves from St. Thomas and St. John, has two 53' twin engine, smooth-riding catamarans (twin-hulled power boats) that each accommodate up to 40 people. Weather permitting, the route is along the north shore of Tortola, on to Virgin Gorda to The Valley to clear customs, to The Baths for swimming and snorkeling, a buffet lunch on board while anchored off Ginger or Salt Island, and then to The Caves for another round of snorkeling. Custom-built to explore the BVI, these comfortable boats have plenty of deck space, two freshwater showers, and large heads (bathrooms). The fee (which includes lunch and open bar) is $90 per adult, $50 for each child under 12 plus a $10 customs fee for each person. Passengers board at Benner Bay just outside of Red Hook. Boats leave at 8am and return about 4:30pm.

STORMY PETREL and **PIRATE'S PENNY** (775-7990) are two 42' diesel single engine power boats which leave from Red Hook in St. Thomas. Each takes a maximum of 12 people. The route, weather permitting, is generally up along the north side of Tortola, over to Virgin Gorda to clear customs in The Valley and then to anchor nearby at The Baths, on to lunch at the restaurant on Cooper Island, then snorkeling at The Indians, and back to Red Hook. The fee for the trip and complimentary open bar is $90 per person (any age) plus a Customs fee of $10. Lunch, which will run about $8 to $20, is additional. Passengers meet at the Blue Marlin no later than 8am and return about 4:30pm.

RUSH HOUR II, a high speed 34' Scarab (just like the Miami Vice boat) and a 38' Cigarette (both 830hp), are available for private charter. If six of you feel like spending $200 each, you can completely customize your trip and visit as many islands as you want. You can even go to Anegada! At 70mph, you can get from Red Hook to The Baths on Virgin Gorda in about 45 minutes (that same trip, just one way, takes all day by sail!). Call **High Performance Charters** (777-7545). The cost is $1200 per day for the Scarab, which includes fuel, Customs fees, and transportation to and from your hotel. Lunch is extra.

PER DOHM WATER TAXI (775-6501) is the place to call if you know you want to go to the the BVI but you don't know exactly where. Just tell them your interests (one of you wants a deserted beach, the other one wants to snorkel, etc.) and they'll tailor-make a trip for you in one of their power catamarans. Their pilot/guides are incredibly knowledgeable and can take you places and show you things most people don't know about -- like the underwater lava flows off of Tortola. Also, if you're not interested in water activities, say so. They can take you to a good hiking spot on a deserted island if you want! They also have scheduled trips to Tortola and The Baths on Virgin Gorda. Inquire.

THE CHARTERBOAT CENTER (775-7990; from the U.S. 800-866-5714), located at the entrance to the Blue Marlin in Red Hook, specializes in trips from St. Thomas to the British Virgin Islands and can arrange a variety of power boat trips, sportsfishing trips, day sails, and even weekly charters. If you're not sure what you want they'll help you decide. Call ahead or stop by their offices. They also have a small retail store where you can buy charts, cruising guides, underwater cameras, film, suntan lotion, and souvenirs.

RENTING YOUR OWN BOAT

Freedom, privacy, and adventure are the primary advantages of renting your own small boat. You decide where to go and how long you want to stay. This can be a great way to explore the beaches and snorkeling areas of the BVI when it is not too windy. You can reach Jost Van Dyke in 30 minutes, the Caves on Norman Island in 45 minutes, and The Baths on Virgin Gorda in 90 minutes.

However, pay attention to the weather. Unless you're an old salt, don't even think of doing this on a really windy day. You'll be wet, scared to death, bounced about, and it will take forever to get anywhere.

Boats rent for a daily rate and come with canopies, charts, radios, ice chests, and snorkel gear. Gas and oil are extra and will run probably somewhere between $12 and $60 depending on whether you are mostly anchored or mostly running the boat the whole time. A captain is an additional $80 to $100.

Clearing Customs: You must clear Customs, which is easy to do. You'll need proof of citizenship (voter's registration card, birth certificate with raised seal, or passport). On Jost Van Dyke, head to the Customs Building at the end of the town dock. On Virgin Gorda, it's at the Yacht Harbour just north of The Baths. Avoid clearing on Tortola as customs offices are located at the West End and Road Town public ferry docks and can be crowded with ferry arrivals.

Virgin Voyages (775-7891), which is run by Betty and Paul Sammis at Sapphire Marina, is at the Sapphire Beach Hotel just north of Red Hook. Their 23' boats with 150 hp engines hold up to six adults. Boats can be rented for consecutive days but cannot be used overnight. They can be picked up as early as 7:30am and are due back at the fuel dock by 4:30pm the same day (or later by special arrangement but never after dark). Rates are $210 for the first day and $185 for the second day (even if it's a year later!) plus gas and oil.

See and Ski (775-6265), at the American Yacht Harbor at Red Hook, rents 22' Makos with 150 hp engines that can hold up to six adults. You are allowed to take the boat overnight or longer provided you have hotel reservations at your destination (for example at Sandcastle on Jost Van Dyke). Boats must be safely secured to a dock or mooring before dark. Rates are $205 a day (lower for three or more days) plus gas and oil.

Nauti Nymph (775-5066), at the American Yacht Harbor in St. Thomas, rents various sizes of deep V-hulled boats with 150, 200, and twin 150 hp engines.

Boats can be rented overnight, but must be secured at a mooring or dock when dark. The daily rate for a 21' boat (up to six people) is $205; for a 25' boat (up to eight people) is $235; and a 27' boat (up to 10 people) is $285. Water skis, snorkeling and fishing gear included. Add $30 for their sleek, high performance Fountain Powerboats.

PUBLIC FERRIES FROM ST. THOMAS

Public ferries travel between the USVI and the BVI, but most ferry schedules don't allow for much sightseeing time as they are mainly for commuters. However, there are important exceptions. Inter-Island Ferry (809-776-6597) runs all the ferries listed below (unless noted).

WEEKEND FERRIES TO JOST VAN DYKE
On Fridays, Saturdays, and Sundays, Inter-Island takes passengers to Jost Van Dyke from Red Hook. Ferries leave Red Hook at 8am, 2pm, and 5:15pm (not on Saturday) and leave Cruz Bay at 8:30am, 2:20pm, and 5:40pm (not on Saturday).The ferry leaves Jost Van Dyke at 9:15am, 3:15pm (except Saturday), and 9:15pm.

FULL-MOON PARTIES
Once a month, and twice when there is a blue moon, Inter-Island ferries leave Red Hook, St. Thomas early in the evening for Bomba's famous all-night Full-Moon Parties on Tortola. The parties spill along the beach and all across the road from this ramshackle beachfront bar and last until way past sunrise. Ferries return to St. Thomas in the morning.

TORTOLA FROM RED HOOK
If you feel like getting up early, the ferry schedule from Red Hook to Tortola does give you time to explore. You can catch a 7:45am ferry (call **Native Son** at 774-8685).The ride takes about half an hour. After you clear Customs, taxi drivers will vie for your attention, so it's best to have plans already made.

If you want to go to a beach, consider taking a taxi over the hill to Long Bay, where you will find a great beach as well as an excellent bar and a casual lunch restaurant at the Long Bay Beach Resort. If you want to shop, have the driver head to Frenchman's Cay, where there is a Pusser's Restaurant and Store plus other clothing shops and art galleries. You can also rent a car. Walk out of Customs, turn left, and walk to the Jolly Roger, where there are Hertz cars for rent. You can easily drive to Long Bay, Cane Garden Bay, and see Road Town and still get back for the 4pm ferry back to Red Hook.

ST. JOHN FOR A DAY

St. John is a great place to plan to spend a day.
Most of the island is a National Park. And it's only
20 minutes by ferry from Red Hook.

What can you do there?

You can hike on trails,
head to beautiful beaches,
follow the underwater snorkel trail
at Trunk Bay,
wander around the little town
of Cruz Bay,
browse through very original shops in one of the
prettiest shopping spots
in the Caribbean – Mongoose Junction,
look for a real mongoose,
rent a car and drive around the island (take
Centerline Road in at least one direction to see
spectacular views),
eat at some excellent restaurants,
take the Reef Bay Trail and see petroglyphs.

KAYAKS AND LITTLE POWER BOATS

The waters off of the east end of St. Thomas are wonderful places to take a little power boat or a kayak and do some exploring. There are lots of coves to visit and a number of nearby little islets that you can motor or paddle to. You can head to the uninhabited cays of Lavango or Mingo and have your own private picnic or you can go over to St. John and take a look at the beautiful beaches there.

KAYAKING

There's nothing but the sound of your paddling when you head out in a kayak. This sport is becoming increasingly popular in the Virgin Islands. **West Indies Wind Surfing** at Vessop Bay Beach (775-6350) rents kayaks by the hour, by the day, and by the week. They are across from the American Yacht Harbor complex and at a particularly good location to begin a kayak trip. They also have kites that you can use to propel you -- but don't let the wind take you too far in one direction, or you'll have a long paddle back.

RENTING A LITTLE POWERBOAT

A number of outfits on the east end of St. Thomas, including **Virgin Voyages**, **Nauti Nymph**, and **See and Ski**, rent little 20' to 25' power boats that you can take out for a day to just go for a ride or to go visit an uninhabited cay or a nearby island. *See page 120 for more specific details .*

SOME OF THE BEST
OF ST. THOMAS
FROM A TO Z

The best ARMAGNACS at Hotel 1829. . .the best BEACH has to be Magen's Bay, even though it's busy. . .the best CONCH FRITTERS at Eunice's Terrace. . .some bests for DAY TRIPS, St. John, Jost, Tortola. . .the best for ELEGANCE, the Grand Palazzo. . . some best FAMILY RESORTS would be the Bolongos, Sugar Bay. . .some of the best GARMENTS (and ties) at Nicole Miller. . .for the best HAT STORE you've got to go to St. John. . . and the best INNKEEPERS are probably Torrie, Bob, and the Borns. . .for great JAZZ it's Blackbeard's. . .and the best KAYAKING is at West Indies Windsurfing. . . and the very best LICORICE at A Chew or Two, of course. . . and the best MASSAGE would be beside the sea. . . for great NIGHTTIME ENTERTAINMENT it's hard to beat the Old Mill. . . the greatest OLIVE BREAD, yep, Zorba's. . . and the best PARASAILING is at the east end. . .the best QUESIDILLAS are at Cafe Sito. . .and the best ROMANTIC LUNCH has got to be Virgilio's. . .and ROMANTIC DINNER Entre Nous. . .the best SPEED BOAT is Rush Hour II, and the most fun TOYS are at Mini Mouse House. . .the easiest UNDERWATER experience is Snuba on St. John. . .the best VIEWS are everywhere on the island...and the best WINE CELLARS can be found at Virgilio's and Epernay and Room with a View. . .the best XERES COCKTAIL at MacKenzie's. . .and maybe the best YOGURT in the world at the Haagen Dazs spot in Red Hook and. . .the best ZUPPA DI CIPOLLE at Romano's Restaurant.

INDEX

1829 Bar 61,124
99 Steps 20
A Chew or Two 71,80,124
Admiral's Inn 31
Adventurer's Club Sports Bar 62
Agave Terrace 27,49
Air Center Helicopters 118
airport (old) 55
Airport Taxis 54
Alexander's Bar and Grill 50
Alexander's Cafe 44
American Airlines 14
American Eagle 66
American Yacht Harbor Deli 56
Animal Crackers 79,80
Arts Alive 108
Asolare 94
Atlantis Submarine 107
Back Street Boutique 73,80
Bad Art Bar 94
Barnacle Bill's 62
Base Clothing 73,80
bathing suits 78
Bay Winds restaurant 28
beaches 99
Beach House 78,80
Bernard K. Passman Gallery 70,80
Big Planet 82
Blackbeard's Castle 32
Blackbeard's Castle Restaurant 46
Blackbeard's Piano Lounge 60,124
black coral jewelry 70
Bolongo Elysian 25
Bomba's 121
books 77,82
Botany Bay Beach 99
Brewer's Bay Beach 99
British Virgin Islands 14,36,117
Bumpa's 89
bugs 112
Burger King 69,89
Cafe Amici 89
Cafe Sagapo 48
Cafe Sito 47,89,124

Cafe Vecchio 24
Calypso 71,80
Camille Pissaro Art Gallery 84
candy 71
car rentals 107
Caribbean items 71
Caribbean para-sailing 97
Caribbean Print Gallery 71,80,84
Caribbean Watersports 97
Carib Health Complex 101
catamaran 66
CDs 77
Charlotte Amalie landmarks 68
Charlotte Amalie shopping 69
Charterboat Center 98,119
Chart House 61
Chili Cookoff 52
Chris Sawyer Dive Center 28,98
Chris Sawyer Diving Store 83
Classics in the Garden 108
clothing 73
Club Elysian Fitness Center 101
Coral World 106
cosmetics 86
Cosmopolitan 73,80
Cowboys and Indians 75,80
Craig and Sally's 47,61
Cuckoo's Nest 74,80
Delta Airlines 14
Dilly D'Alley 78,80
Dockside Books 82
Dohm Water Taxi 93
Dolphin Airlines 65
Down Island Traders 71,80
Drake's Seat 107
East End 17
Eileen's Cookies 90
Elizabeth James 83
Ellington's 94
Emancipation Garden 105
entertainment 66
Entre Nous Restaurant 43,124
Epernay 59,124
Eunice's Terrace 51,124
Fashion Eyewear 78,80
Fast Cat 66
Fast Ferries 66

Fish Trap 94
fitness 101
Mahogany Run 101
Fort Christian 105
Frank's Bake Shop 56
Frederick Gallery 84
Frederick Lutheran Church 105
Frenchman's Reef 26
Frenchtown 17,56
Frenchtown Coffee House 50
Frenchtown Deli 56
full-moon parties 121
Gallow's Point 94
games 79
gifts 76
Gladys' Cafe 51
glasses 78
Gold's Gym 101
golf 101
Grand Palazzo 24,124
Grass Cay 18
Grateful Deli 56
great sights 19
green flash 37,94
Greenhouse 62,89
Gucci 76,80
Haagen Dazs Bakery 56,124
Hard Rock Cafe 89
Hardwood Cafe 90
Hassel Island 113,114
Havensight shopping 82
Hill Aviation 118
Hook Line and Sinker 50
Hotel 1829 33
Hotel 1829 Restaurant 43
Hull Bay Beach 99
hydrofoil 66
I Cappuccini 90
I Frati 76,80
Ice Cream Shoppe 91
Il Cardinale 44
inns 31
Island Beachcomber 30
Island Newsstand 77,80
Janine's Boutique 74,80
jazz 60
jet skis 97

Katran I,II 66
kayaks 97,123
Ken Done 74,80
Kilnworks Pottery 84
Land of Oz 79,80
Le Badesse Boutique 74,80
leather 77
Leather Store 77,80
Light Bites 91
Limestone Reef Terraces 114
Limnos Charters 118
Lindbergh Beach 99
Lindquist Beach 100
Little St. James 108
Little Treasures 76,80
Local Color 72,74,80
Lookout Bar 61
machineel tree 38
Mackenzie's 62
Mad Max 97
magazines 77
Magen's Bay Beach 100,124
Mango Tango Art Gallery 84
Marina Market 56,83
Mariott's Frenchman's Reef 26,101
Marriott's Morning Star 26
McLaughlin Anderson 35,111
Mini Mouse House Toys 79,80,124
Modern Music 82
Mongoose Restaurant 94
Morning Star Beach 100
Morning Star Resort 26
Mountain Top 107
Music Shoppe 77,80
Name Dropper 74,80
National Historic Landmark 32
National Historic Site 33
Nauti Nymph 120,123
newspapers 77
Nicole Miller Boutique 72,76,80,124
North Side 18
Old Mill 62,124
Old Mill Restaurant 49
Old Stone House 46
Palm Passage Cafe 90
Palm Terrace 24,45
Paradise Point Tram 107

Paradiso 94
parasailing 97
passport 14
Pavilions and Pools 34
pedal boats 97
Per Dohm Water Taxi 93,119
phosphorus 37
Pirate's Penny 119
Point Pleasant Resort 27
Polli's 108
Post Office 68
public ferries 121
Puerto Rico 14
Purses and Things 77,80
Pusser's 94
Pusser's Candy Store 83
Pusser's Company Store 72,75,80
Puzzles Bar 63
Red Hook 17,56
Red Hook shopping 82
Reichhold Center Gallery 84
Renaissance Grand Beach 28
Renaissance Grand Beach Resort 101
resorts 23
restaurants 41
Romano's 45,61,124
Room with a View 59,124
Rush Hour II 119,124
sandals 78
Sapphire Beach 100
Satori Pottery 83
Scott Beach 100 •
scuba diving 98
Seaborne Seaplane Adventures 66,117
seaplane 66
See and Ski 120,123
Seven Arches Museum 106
Seychelles 94
Shipwreckers 76,80
shoes 78
Shoe Tree 78,80
Shooting stars 37
shopping 67
shopping finds 72
shopping map 18
size of St. Thomas 13
Smith Bay Beach 100

snorkeling 98
Soft Touch Boutique 75,80
St. Croix 13,14,65
St. John 36,93
St. Thomas location 13,14,38
Stateside newspapers 36
Stormy Petrel 119
Sugar Bay 29
sunglasses 78
swimwear 78
Synagogue 105
tapes 77
taxi drivers 53
taxi tips 53
taxis 53
Thatch Cay 18
The Blue Marlin 48
The Gallery 84
Tickles 62,113
Tillet Gardens 84,108
Tortola 14,121
toys 79
Upstairs Gallery 84
Vessup Bay Beach 97,100,123
villas 35
Virgilio's 42,61,91,124
Virgilio's Wine Cellar 60,124
Virgin Island Hydrofoil Services 66
Virgin Islands National Park 114
Virgin Voyages 120,123
Water Bay Beach 100
Water Island 113
waverunners 97
West End 18
West Indian food 20
West Indies' Coffee 90
West Indies Wind Surfing 97,123,124
Windjammer 61
windsurfing 98
Wyndham Sugar Bay 29,101
Zelda's Stand 91
Zora's 78,80
Zorba's 48,56,90,124

ABOUT THE AUTHOR

Ms. Acheson's *The Best of St. Thomas* is the second of a series. *The Best of the British Virgin Islands* was the first, and *The Best of Anguilla* will soon be the third.

After a "lifetime" in New York City Ms. Acheson decided the boardroom had turned into the "bored room" for her. She and her husband then made the move from Manhattan. They "traded" Manhattan Island for an island off the coast of Florida and the islands of the Caribbean -- where they now divide their time.

Along with her own books and her consulting to several worldwide travel services, Ms. Acheson is also a regular contributor to *Fodor's Caribbean*, *Fodor's Affordable Caribbean*, *Fodor's Virgin Islands*, *Fodor's Florida*, *Fodor's Affordable Florida*, and *Fodor's Cruises and Ports of Call*. Her articles and photographs have appeared in local and national publications including *Travel and Leisure*, *Caribbean Travel and Life*, and *Florida Travel and Life*.

Ms. Acheson is quite happy with the "trade."